Carshalton House in Surry, the Seat of Theodore Henry Broadhead Esq[r].

The 1783 view by W. Watts.

The story of Carshalton House

A.E. Jones

London Borough of Sutton Libraries and Arts Services

ILLUSTRATIONS ACKNOWLEDGMENTS

Pages vi, 64: photos by Roy Van Dyke.

Map, page 4, by kind permission of His Grace the Duke of Norfolk.

Pages 11, 95: photos by Graham Prothero, by kind permission of the Daughters of the Cross.

Pages 13, 49, from Field, H and Bunney, M. *English Domestic Architecture of the XVIIth and XVIIIth Centuries*, Bell, 1905.

Pages 33 (top), 66, 90: photos by Douglas Cluett, by kind permission of the Daughters of the Cross.

Page 43: from drawings made by Sister Pauline Stevens; but the responsibility for the annotations is entirely the author's.

Page 56: from *The Universal Museum and Complete Magazine* for 1765 (via Sister Pauline Stevens).

Page 76: Photos by George Jenkinson (bowl in care of Sutton Libraries and Arts Services).

Page 89 (bottom): Photo by Frank Burgess.

Pages (a) 33 (top), 99, 101, 107 and (b) 85, 89 (top); prints by Frank Burgess from glass plates in the (a) Knights Whittome and (b) Francis collections in Sutton Libraries' Local Collection.

Page 114: from a copy made by Sister Pauline Stevens.

Copies of these pictures are in Sutton Libraries' Local Collection; as are the other illustrations used.

GRAPHICS AND DESIGN: SHIRLEY EDWARDS

First Published 1980

London Borough of Sutton Libraries and Arts Services
Central Library, St. Nicholas Way, Sutton, Surrey
Tel. 01-661 5050
© Text: A. E. Jones

ISBN 0 907335 01 2

Printed by Dasprint Ltd., 159 Brookwood Road, London SW18.

PREFACE

A few of the historical facts in this book come from the standard works on Surrey, but, unfortunately, much of what they say about Carshalton House is inaccurate, and the truth has to be gathered, very largely, from unpublished material and incidental references in publications on other subjects. I did not, however, have to discover the existence of all these sources of information by my own efforts. The way to some of my researches was pointed by Mr. C. R. B. Barrett, a late 19th century owner-historian of the premises, by Dr. A. V. Peatling, who brought so much of Carshalton's past to light, and by Sister Dominic Savio (Marjorie Scofield), who, in an article printed in Vol. 65 of the Surrey Archaeological Collections, referred to certain very revealing documents in the Surrey Record Office, which were not catalogued until 1959. But my greatest debt of gratitude is owed to another Daughter of the Cross, Sister Pauline Stevens, who, when she was at Carshalton House, embarked on a very extensive investigation into its past, and has most generously made the fruits of her labours available to me. Specific references in the text make fuller acknowledgement of what her discoveries have contributed to my history of this very interesting 'Queen Anne' mansion, which, after passing through the hands of some fifteen owners in the space of a little less than 200 years, has for nearly 90 years now, belonged to the Daughters of the Cross.

I must also express my sincere thanks to Mr. D. J. Cluett, Principal Librarian, Reference Information Services, to the London Borough of Sutton, who encouraged me to write this book and helped in its preparation in every possible way. I would also like to acknowledge the help with design and graphics given by Shirley Edwards.

Muslims are said always to introduce a deliberate fault into any work they undertake, because only Allah can achieve perfection. I have never myself found it necessary to resort to that device in order to avoid a seeming pretension to impeccability; and I feel sure that errors and omissions will be found in the text of this book. If so, they are entirely my responsibility; all who have helped me did their best to prevent me making mistakes.

The south and east façades. The buildings seen beyond the house are twentieth century.

CHAPTER ONE
The history of the site

There can be few plots of land in Britain whose whole history is known with certainty, and, in the case of a mansion like Carshalton House with grounds formed out of a number of separate medieval enclosures, it is not to be expected that the former uses made of those will ever be discovered completely. This particularly applies to the area round the entrance gates to the carriage drive. Referring to the latter's construction, Aubrey's *Antiquities of Surrey*, published in 1718, said that Sir John Fellowes (who had recently acquired Carshalton House) "in levelling the Road to make a handsom Avenue to his Seat, discovered a great Quantity of Bones, mostly human". It turned out that he had not exhausted the area's possibilities in this respect. Some seventy years later, James Edwards, in *A Companion from London to Brightelmston* added to Aubrey's account the information that "only a few years since, in removing of earth near the entrance gates, a large quantity of bones was likewise discovered". And, when a tree close to those same gates blew down in February 1974, there were found beneath its roots yet more human bones.

No record or memory has survived to suggest what event or events could have accounted for all those corpses. In Aubrey's book it is surmised that the site had been "formerly a Caemitory or that it was a Field of Battle". But Carshalton's church is as old as Domesday Book and was probably in existence on the same site well before the Norman Conquest, so there can hardly have been a Christian graveyard at this spot — unless, of course, it was one used in pre-Saxon times by a Romano-British church which was subsequently completely destroyed during the Anglo-Saxon invasions. Was it then one of the invading race's burial grounds before it accepted Christianity? Or do the bones date back to a much more remote era when the native inhabitants themselves were pagans?

Examination of the 1974 find by experts from the Surrey Archaeological Society established that it contained the long bones of an adult and the jaw of a seven year old child. But the remains had been much disturbed and damaged by the roots of the tree, and only very incomplete skeletons were recovered. In the soil over the bones there was a quantity of building rubble, together with some pottery fragments dating from the 13th to the 16th century — and also a medieval key. The building rubble was what one would expect to find in the foundations of a carriage drive, but such an extensive time-spread for the pottery is puzzling. It

1

is possible that all the rubbish came from the demolition of the medieval mansion which is known to have preceded Carshalton House on or near its site. But, in the end, all that can be said with certainty is that the human interments pre-dated the planting of the tree — which means only that they took place at least 200 years ago. In all the circumstances, however, they are likely to have been of very much greater antiquity. A systematic 'dig' of the whole area round the entrance gates is impracticable because they are in constant use, so the origins of the Carshalton House boneyard will probably remain for ever a complete mystery. We have not even an exact description of what was found in the 18th century to suggest a solution.

With regard to the idea that an ancient battlefield may lie just inside the gates of Carshalton House, it can only be said that there is no record of any battle ever having taken place anywhere on Carshalton's soil. And a child of seven seems an unlikely casualty in anything but a most brutal massacre. On the other hand, it must be said that, in earlier times, there were probably many tribal slaughters of which no record has survived — or was even made.

Leaving behind the fascinating but booby-trapped fields of historical specu-lation, it is to the medieval records of the Manor of Carshalton that one must go for the earliest authentic information about the Carshalton House site. The Court Rolls show that, when John Scott died in 1533, he was the owner of a "Capital Messuage with certain Lands belonging called Kenwardesle", which had formerly belonged to Edward Burton. The latter in 1507 had sold to John Scott the Manor of Kinnersley (to use the later standardised spelling of the name) comprising two messuages, 100 acres of land, 40 acres of meadow, 100 acres of pasture and 10 acres of wood in Carshalton, Sutton, Morden and Wallington. And it emerges from later entries in the Court Rolls that the "Capital Messuage" which went with the Manor of Kinnersley was called The Old Farm, the earliest owner of which to be mentioned in those entries was Bartholomew Kynardsley. It is probable then that The Old Farm was built by him; but the only thing on record about him is that in 1362 he was fined by the manorial court for allowing some of his hogs to get into the lord's fields.

John Scott, owner of The Old Farm and the Manor of Kinnersley from 1507 to 1533, was a Baron (i.e. judge) of the Exchequer Court in Henry VIII's reign. (And it is indicative of the attraction that a country residence in Carshalton had in earlier ages for Londoners of wealth and distinction that another Baron of the Exchequer Court, Christopher Muschamp, was contemporaneously living in the Stone Court mansion). John Scott's heir was a son of the same name, but eventually the Carshalton property had to be divided among five Scott brothers. With its lands spread over four parishes, the Manor of Kinnersley had always been a very 'synthetic' territorial unit, and its claimed manorial status probably dated to the time when any landowner with two tenants bound by feudal obligations to him could call his holding a manor, while still himself having to swear fealty to the lords of the original manors within whose boundaries his properties lay. The 'rights' appertaining to such sub-manors became pretty well worthless if they had to be divided among a number of individuals; and, though fractions of the Manor of Kinnersley continued to pass nominally with land transfers until 1683, after that all trace of it is lost. The territory which went with it remained a reality; and so did The Old Farm. But it is impossible now to establish exactly what area continued to go with the house — though old land deeds show that the total acreage was quite considerable.

To modern ears The Old Farm does not sound like the name of a 'Capital Messuage', as the old legal phraseology had it. But a 'farm', originally, was a land holding in respect of which the owner had been excused all feudal obligations in return for a yearly payment of money. That, in early medieval times, would have been a privilege granted only to members of the aristocracy. (In the Court Rolls The Old Farm is described as a "free" capital messuage, yielding a rent of 38s. per annum — a considerable sum in those days.) And it is clear from the social position of 17th century occupiers of the premises that those still retained then the status of a 'gentleman's residence'. By local standards, the house was certainly quite a large one. In 1664 it was assessed to tax on 10 hearths — a number equalled by Stone Court and exceeded only by the mansion called Mascalls in Carshalton Park and one other which cannot now be identified.

A little earlier in the century The Old Farm had been good enough to bring to Carshalton Sir Edward Herbert, Attorney General to Charles I during the last years of that monarch's reign. In view of his very eminent legal status it is sad to record that Sir Edward Herbert figures in the Court Rolls of the Carshalton manor mainly as an alleged stopper-up of public rights of way. (But it may be some excuse that his royal master had not set a good example in caring for other people's rights). Looking at the high brick wall which, for nearly three centuries, has guarded the Carshalton House estate on the south and east, it is difficult to imagine the appearance of the site before the wall was built. But old land deeds make it clear that the present park was originally a collection of medieval fields, with names like Chalkhill, Spring Close, Roomes and the Little Pightle, through which there ran a particularly important public right of way.

The situation which Sir Edward Herbert faced is indicated on the 'Arundel' map of Carshalton. Why 'Arundel'? Well, in 1621 the dowager Countess of Arundel purchased half the manor of Carshalton, and in due course this moiety passed to her grandson, Henry, Earl of Arundel. After his death, his executors sold it in 1659, but a map of Carshalton remained in the Arundel archieves. When this map came to be catalogued in modern times, some words on it led to its being taken for a map of Beddington, and it was dated, by the style of the handwriting, to about 1670. Not until comparatively recently was its true character discovered; and now, divorced as it is from any contemporary documentation, neither its exact date nor the professional status of its maker can be established. Even more impossible of verification is how accurately and completely, it depicts the Carshalton of its time. Two obvious defects in it are that, among the buildings it shows, there is neither a house corresponding to The Old Farm nor a mansion in Carshalton Park, although both are known to have existed long before the Arundel acquisition of half the manor. The explanation of this may well be that the map was primarily intended to indicate the parts of Carshalton owned or controlled by the Arundels, and the rest of the area was only perfunctorily sketched in. It is noticeable that field boundaries are marked in some areas but not in others.

However, if on general geographical features the Arundel map may be accepted at its face value, some very interesting facts emerge about the structure of 17th century Carshalton, one of them being that the contemporary West Street, at its southern end, before reaching Pound Street, curved sharply south-

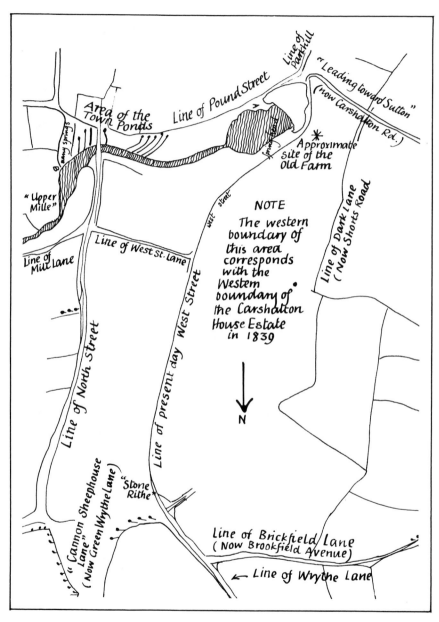

The map contains the following labels:

- Line of Park Hill
- "Leading toward Sutton" (now Carshalton Rd.)
- Line of Pound Street
- Area of the Town Ponds
- Bonny Springs
- the Island
- Approximate site of the Old Farm
- "Upper Mille"
- Line of West St. Lane
- Line of Dark Lane (Now Shorts Road)
- Line of Mill Lane
- NOTE The western boundary of this area corresponds with the Western boundary of the Carshalton House Estate in 1839
- West Street
- N
- Line of North Street
- Line of present day West Street
- "Cannon Shephouse Lane" (Now Green Wrythe Lane)
- "Stone Rithe"
- Line of Brickfield Lane (Now Brookfield Avenue)
- Line of Wrythe Lane

Central portion of the 'Arundel' map (see Chapter One). The words originally on the map are shown in quotation marks. NOTE: Compare the boundary lines shown here with those on the 1839 Estate Plan on page 114.

4

westwards, skirting the north side of the Carshalton House lake and joining the road to Sutton roughly opposite the present-day 'Windsor Castle'. This route was bound to have passed close by The Old Farm, even allowing for the fact that the lake, as drawn on the 'Arundel' map, is very unlike the existing one both in shape and orientation. The waters depicted beyond it also bear no resemblance to those of modern times; there is, for instance, nothing corresponding to Margaret's Well, and the town ponds are represented only by a hatched area marked "Many springs". In fact, the outfall of the Carshalton House lake is shown as the sole source of the Carshalton Wandle, flowing on as a single stream to join the "Beddington River" just up-stream of the old Hack Bridge. Can this picture of Carshalton in the first half of the 17th century really be true? It is impossible now to be sure, but it would certainly help to explain some puzzling things in the history of the village. It would also account for the strong resistance to the stopping up by Sir Edward Herbert of the footpath which the Court Rolls described as "leading through a close called Hill Close from the West Street towards Sutton". The 'Arundel' map shows no highway from West Street to its present junction with Pound Street; the lake and its outfall offer an apparently unbridged watery barrier across the modern road. And, without the footpath past The Old Farm, the traveller from West Street would seemingly have had to make a long detour if going to Sutton.

Identification of the right of way stopped up by Sir Edward Herbert with the old southwestward extension of West Street is made pretty certain by its having gone through "Hill Close". "Hilly Close" is particularised in a land deed of 1656 as a 1½ acre plot abutting on "Ames Ace [sic] on the south, The Old Farme on the north, Spring Close on the east and the footway from Carshalton to Sutton on the west". Furthermore, the Court Rolls for 1691 mention "the Pond abutting on Spring Close" as an appurtenance of The Old Farm; and the 'Arundel' map has the words "Spring head" written against the southern end of the Carshalton House lake.

I am greatly indebted to Sister Pauline Stevens for drawing my attention to the significance of all these details and for pointing out also that the "Grove Wilderness" mentioned as a land holding of 18th century owners of Carshalton House was not, as I had assumed, in the present grounds of 'The Grove' mansion, but was a joining together of Chalkhill, Spring Close, Roomes, Little Pightle and most of Craddocks to transform what was previously agricultural land into a feature in a gentleman's park. (My misconception about the geographical situation of the "Grove Wilderness", incidentally, invalidated an inference I drew in 'An illustrated directory of old Carshalton' concerning the site of the former vicarage).

It is not clear whether Sir Edward Herbert reopened the footpath to Sutton or simply took no notice of the manorial court (which, as an institution, had, by this time, lost much of its old power and prestige). The villagers had certainly taken on a formidable legal opponent. The great Lord Clarendon, a contemporary of Sir Edward's but not an admirer, though on the same side politically, wrote of him that he was "the proudest man living" and that "his greatest faculty was, and in which he was a master, to make difficult things more intricate and perplexed, and very easy things to seem more hard than they were".

Sir Edward Herbert joined the King in Oxford after the outbreak of the Civil War, and in 1646 Parliament included him in a list of persons "incapable of pardon" and, in consequence, his estates were confiscated. Following the execution of Charles I, Sir Edward fled to the Hague, where the future Charles II renewed his appointment as Attorney General. But he was never again to hold that office in England and did not live to see the Restoration, dying in Paris in 1657.

His successor in The Old Farm was another lawyer, Dixey Longe, who presumably had the authority of Parliament for his acquisition. Dixey Longe also bought half the manor of Carshalton (not the 'Arundel' half) and, in later land deeds, "The Manor House" is given as an alternative name for The Old Farm. This seems to have resulted from Dixey Longe's occupation of the premises and there is no evidence that the alternative name dated back to the time when they went with the Manor of Kinnersley. At any rate, the owner of the other half of the Carshalton manor had called his house "The Manor House" when he sold it to the Countess of Arundel, and Dixey Longe had just as much right to confer the title on his dwelling place.

In 1656, shortly after the new owner of The Old Farm had come to live in Carshalton, the Court Rolls registered a complaint that he had stopped up the footpath from West Street through Hill Close. This may have been an attempt to get Dixey Longe to remedy an already existing infringement of a public right; but whether or not the footpath was subsequently reopened does not appear. All that can be said is that it is not recorded again as a bone of contention. The possibility cannot be excluded that Dixey Longe provided an alternative route which would keep the public well clear of his house. It is certain that by 1720 a causeway alongside the boundary of the Carshalton House estate had come into existence to give pedestrian access from West Street to its present junction with Pound Street (but horse traffic still had to go through water). When this causeway was made is not, however, recorded in any surviving document.

Unlike Sir Edward Herbert, Dixey Longe did not commit himself fervently to either King or Parliament. He flourished under the rule of both Charles I and Cromwell, and he survived the Restoration with undiminished status, dying in 1664, four years after Charles II had returned to his inheritance. Dixey Longe had been admitted to Lincoln's Inn in 1634, and, although his father was an 'armiger' (i.e. entitled to armorial bearings), he was a third son, so his success in life was probably largely due to his own efforts. He was certainly a wealthy man when he died, and he left his widow, Theodosia, well provided for with a life interest in most of his estate. In his will he, rather touchingly, explained that "all this is due to her inasmuch as when she was young and beautiful, and of an honourable family, and had plentiful fortune, she took me to be her husband without any condition of my provision of any maintenance or joynture whatsoever."

Theodosia (who Sister Pauline Stevens discovered, from the Court Rolls, was a Dallyson) had a marble monument placed in Carshalton church, commemorating her late husband as "a man approved for his fidelity, diligence and prudence, especially conspicuous for attention to his religious duties, the courteousness of his manners, the moderation of his desires, distinguished for his kindness towards the deserving, his charity towards the poor, his justice to all men." The inscription concluded "In the 54th year of his age, after he had prepared himself for a better life with much diligence and patience, he calmly gave up his soul to God." There is nothing in all this to suggest that Dixey Longe would have been a trampler on the rights of humble villagers; but, of course,

6

disputes over footpaths do not normally get mentioned in epitaphs.

Theodosia did not remain inconsolable. In fact, she seems to have had a successor to Dixey Longe already lined up; for on the 10th October 1664 — exactly six weeks after his death — a licence was granted by the Archbishop of Canterbury for her marriage with Thomas Arden. The only further information to be obtained from the 'Allegations' recorded by the Faculty Office is that the address of Thomas Arden was "the City of Westminster" and he was a bachelor, 37 years of age, while Theodosia, aged 40, was then living in Parmenton, Kent. The wedding took place in the City church of St. Bartholomew the Less and was, no doubt, a quiet one, in the circumstances. But tongues must have wagged furiously when the news became generally known. One cannot help wondering whether Theodosia's memorial to Dixey was in the nature of an apology prompted by a feeling of guilt. It is even possible that his many virtues had made him really a bit difficult to live with, and the "moderation of his desires" may not have been in all respects a recommendation.

I have not been able to discover anything about Thomas Arden's social background or whether he had any money of his own. But, by the law of the time, he became the owner of all his wife's property; and in 1666 his name replaced Dixey Longe's in the 'Hearth Tax' lists — undoubtedly in respect of The Old Farm. In 1683 the Court Rolls also recorded him as being the holder of half the Manor of Carshalton, and that again was almost certainly because of his wife's inheritance from her first husband.

Theodosia died in 1686, but the Carshalton burial register shows that Thomas Arden lived on until 1707. At some unknown time in the late 17th or early 18th century, and by some unknown transaction, The Old Farm came into the possession of Edward Carleton, who, after the death of his first wife (Elisabeth, daughter of Josiah Dewye, owner of Carshalton's gunpowder mills) had, in 1683, married Mary Skinner of Carshalton. This couple had their eldest son baptised Arden and they gave the name Theodosia to one of their daughters. But the nature of the close relationship which evidently existed between the Ardens and the Carletons does not appear from the records. No doubt, however, it facilitated the transfer of The Old Farm to Edward Carleton. The identity of the premises he acquired is unquestionably established by land deeds relating to Carshalton House (now in the Surrey Record Office) which describe it as built "in or near the place where formerly stood the Messuage called the Manner House or Old Farm, all or most part of which before-mentioned premises were heretofore the Estate of Thomas Arden Esq."

Edward Carleton built the Carshalton House we now see, and The Old Farm disappeared except for what seems to have been a portion of one of its walls. That fragment of masonry is constructed of chalk blocks in which are set small squares of flint, forming a chequered pattern calculated to have given a most attractive appearance to the house in its prime. (It is significant that pieces of chalk blocks were found among the rubble over the bones unearthed in 1974.) Chalk and flints were standard building materials in medieval Carshalton where they were locally quarried. A few examples of this style of construction have survived by good fortune, but why the small relic of The Old Farm was not demolished with the rest of the building is a mystery; and, unfortunately, there is no means of telling where in the mansion it was situated. Although I have found no mention of it prior to the late 19th century its significance was well appreciated then. One of the Sisters of St. Philomena's told me that, when the Daughters of the Cross first took over Carshalton House, they were authoritatively advised that this bit of walling was something very special and no harm should be allowed to come to it. So, when the Convent's school was extended over the site, this last fragment of The Old Farm was incorporated in one of the new buildings. There, though not easily seen nowadays, it is at least safely preserved. With the exception of parts of Carshalton church and its precincts, this piece of gray and white chequered wall is probably the oldest bit of masonry now standing in the village.

It seems, however, that in the late 19th century, it had a companion piece because Charles Barrett, who then owned the house, wrote (in notes now in Sutton's Central Library) "... at the back of the house. But beyond this there are two fragments of walls (or were) made of alternate squares of flints and chalk." Barrett also wrote that, behind the present house, "Now and again even the foundations of ancient red brick walls have been uncovered. Bricks appear soft & very fine & red & set in a white mortar in which large lumps of fat are still remaining"; and he clearly thought that these were relics of the previous house. But putting a date on old red bricks and mortar is a job for experts, and, even then, may be largely guess-work. It is known that there were outbuildings of the present mansion which have long since disappeared, and what Charles Barrett saw may have been their foundations.

As was remarked at the beginning of this chapter, the full facts about all that previously existed on the Carshalton House site are never likely to be known.

CHAPTER TWO

The building of Carshalton House

It is only fairly recently that the truth about the building of Carshalton House has been generally known, and old misconceptions on the matter are still current. When, in the late 18th century, Manning and Bray wrote their very scholarly history of Surrey, they said: "Dr. Ratcliffe, the physician, built a house here . . . . His house was sold for £3,500 to Sir John Fellowes, Sub-Governor of the South Sea Company, by whom it was rebuilt." The learned authors had evidently never heard of Edward Carleton in connection with Carshalton House. Nor had Dr. Lysons and Brayley, who each wrote authoritative accounts of Surrey; they both had Fellowes pulling down and rebuilding Radcliffe's creation. Brightling's *'History of Carshalton'*, published in 1872 and proclaiming itself to be "Compiled from the best Authorities", introduced Carleton into the story but got no nearer the truth. According to Brightling, "The earliest record we have of this mansion is that it was built by Dr. Radcliffe"; but he did not say what that record was. Instead, he went on: "It appears that this house became the property of Edward Carleton Esq., and, being seized by the Crown soon afterwards for a debt, was sold with certain lands for the sum of £7,663 to John Fellowes." To make Carleton an owner subsequent to Dr. Radcliffe was, in fact, to turn history upside down.

The *Victoria County History*, published some thirty years later, followed the earlier writers in not mentioning Edward Carleton at all in what it had to say about Carshalton House; it simply named the first proprietor as Dr. Radcliffe and then said that, after his death, the premises were bought by Sir John Fellowes. Even as late as 1949, when the erudite Mr. Derek Sherborn published an article about Carshalton House in *Country Life*, he did not get its history quite right. "The Carleton family", he wrote, "owned the property until 1714 when it was seized for debt, and in May of that year it was purchased for £3,500 by Dr. John Radcliffe . . . . Not long after his death it was sold by his trustees to John Fellowes." So far, so not too bad. But then Mr. Sherborn went on: "He pulled down the old house and built the present one . . . *[which]* in some respects is rather old-fashioned for its time." The reason for its seeming "old-fashionedness" was that, in fact, it had not been built in Sir John Fellowes's time, but in Edward Carleton's.

The origin of all the mistakes about Carshalton House seems to have been a statement in Aubrey's *Natural History and Antiquities of Surrey*, which was published in 1718 after having been brought up to date by Richard Rawlinson twenty years after Aubrey's death. Referring to John Fellowes in Carshalton, the book said that he "is now about building a handsom Seat." After that contemporary testimony, everybody was convinced that Fellowes was responsible for the present mansion. And when I came to write my own history of Carshalton under the title *"From medieval manor to London suburb"*, I put too much trust in the best authorities and stated: "John Fellows immediately *[after his purchase]* set about building a fine new mansion and the old Carleton house was pulled down." It was not until I was gathering material for *An illustrated directory of old Carshalton*, that I discovered the truth about the Carshalton House we now see. A Sister of the Convent there, who had made some researches into the subject, told me of land deeds in the Surrey Record Office which showed that it was really Edward Carleton who had built the still standing mansion. And though those documents do not completely reveal its early history, two inventories taken in the early 18th century make it clear that, after it became Sir John Fellowes's home, it was not rebuilt by him, but altered only in minor respects. The land deeds do not, however, mention Dr. Radcliffe's occupancy of the premises, and the reason for that will appear in Chapter Four.

There are, unfortunately, no records of the actual construction of Carshalton House. The only documentary evidence which bears on that point is, firstly, an averment in court proceedings against Edward Carleton in 1713 that he already owned the premises in April 1710, and, secondly, a statement in the conveyance of 1716 to John Fellowes (he did not get his baronetcy until 1719) that what he was acquiring was "All that Capital Messuage or Mansion house wherein Edward Carleton, late of London, Merchant, lately dwelt . . . lately erected and new Built by the said Edward Carleton." As to what exactly was meant by "lately erected and new Built", all that can be said is that an early 18th century wall painting in one of the mansion's old 'Parlours' shows a royal yacht bearing the initials "A.R." and displaying an ensign which dates to before the Union of England and Scotland in 1707. It is not a historical event which is depicted, and Fellowes, who did not acquire the premises until after Queen Anne's death, is not likely to have commissioned an out-of-date picture; so the presumption is that the wall panel in question is contemporary with Edward Carleton's decoration of the room. (The discovery about the ship's markings was another made by Sister Pauline Stevens, who did what, apparently, nobody previously had thought of doing, and mounted a ladder to make a close inspection of the details of the picture, which was painted very high up on the wall).

As to who the architect of Carshalton House was, there is, in the surviving documents, not a clue; which has not stopped speculation on the subject. The *Victoria County History* boldly asserted that the house was "built by Leoni, but has been robbed of all architectural features"; but it gave no authority for either of those statements. Leoni was, in fact, still living in Italy when Carshalton House was built. (One of the consequences of assuming that Fellowes was responsible for it has been that likely architects have been looked for in the wrong decade.) Field and Bunney in their *English Domestic Architecture of the 17th and 18th Centuries* said of 'Wrencote' in Croydon that it "has so many points in common with Carshalton House that it is reasonable to suppose that they both came from

The marine picture in the Painted Parlour, possibly by Isaac Sailmaker. The large vessel on the right is a 'first rate' (man-of-war)

the same hand. The section of the cornice is very similar, and the return modillions to the inner breaks over the pilasters are omitted, exactly as at Carshalton. The pilasters themselves and the treatment of the sills have also a strong relationship to those of the larger house". Mr. Mervyn E. Macartney, Surveyor to the Fabric of St. Paul's Cathedral, also expressed the opinion in the Architectural Press's *Practical Exemplar* that Carshalton House was designed by the same person as Wrencote "or the same master-craftsmen were employed on both. The influence of Sir Christopher Wren is so strong as to suggest that either the architect or the master-craftsmen were very familiar with his work". (But what architect or master craftsman of the time could have failed to be familiar with the work of the builder of St. Paul's Cathedral?)

However, a big snag lies in the way of the theory that the same person was responsible for the design of both Carshalton House and Wrencote. The latter is confidently dated to between 1715 and 1720, and the architect to whom it is nowadays confidently attributed is Henry Joynes. But he, until 1715, was busily engaged on Blenheim Palace as Vanburgh's assistant and would not have been available to do work for Edward Carleton earlier in the century.

Actually, the style of both Carshalton House and Wrencote is not so much individual as characteristic of the period. In their time both would have seemed merely conventionally fashionable — somewhat like a modern concrete block would to us; and however much appearances may be to the contrary, not every example of that latter style of building has come from the same drawing board. It is even possible that Carshalton House was built by a master mason to general specifications formulated by Edward Carleton himself. Eighteenth century residences were not invariably planned by professional architects. Some gentlemen of the time designed mansions; and so, quite frequently, did master masons.

There is, in fact, nothing complicated in the structure of Carshalton House. It is, basically, a simple rectangular building having on each of three floors nine windows on the long sides and seven on the short ones, the top storey windows being about half the height of those in the lower two storeys. The foundation of the house is a basement, the room plan of which is repeated on the floors above. In the centre of the south front a shallow flight of stone steps leads up to what used to be the principal entrance and still retains its 18th century, carved wooden, pedimented porch supported by 'classical' columns. The east front, too, has a central doorway, similarly approached, but without a porch, though the architrave is richly ornamented and there is a carved panel over it. Both flights of steps appear to have kept their original wrought iron guard rails.

The stock brickwork of the building gives it a tawny colour, but a contrast is introduced by edgings of red brick to the projecting parts of the frontages and to the windows. (Edward Carleton owned one of Carshalton's two 18th century brickyards, and, though he did not work it himself, some of the bricks in Carshalton House may possibly have been made in it.) The façades of the mansion are further saved from monotony, on the long south front, by shallow two-windowed insets extending the whole height of the building on each side of a central block of three windows, with single windows at the two ends; while, on the east side, there is a similar arrangement, minus the single end windows. And, to counterbalance the vertical accents of the tall windows on the lower two floors, projecting courses separate the storeys, culminating in a very wide, heavily carved,

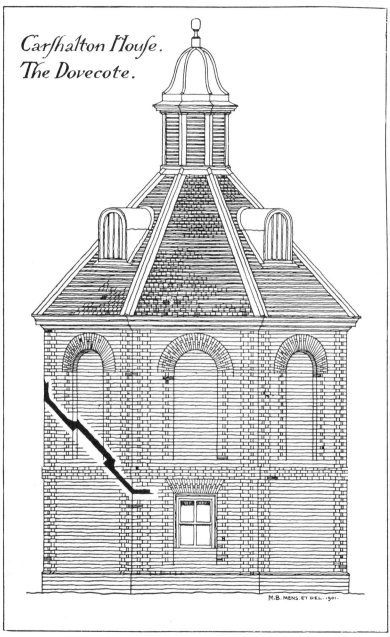

Carfhalton Houfe.
The Dovecote.

M.B. MENS. ET DEL. 1901.

The Dovecote. The thick black line indicates a section of one of the octagonal sides.

13

wooden cornice just below the attics — which gives the latter rather the appearance of an after-thought in the design. But, apart from the somewhat incongruous effect produced by this boldly outthrust cornice, the proportions of Carshalton House are admirable; and the restrained and simple methods by which it charms the eye show its designer — whoever he was — to have been a man of skill and discernment. As the *Victoria County History* said, in its refined and dignified way, "the elevations are refined and dignified."

When Edward Carleton became bankrupt in 1713 the Carshalton House estate was listed as "One capital messuage, five barns, three stables, one dovehouse, three acres of meadow, an acre and a half of garden, three acres of orchard, one wilderness and five fish ponds" (the latter covering approximately four acres). What was almost certainly the original dovecote still existed early in this century, and was the subject of an illustration in the already mentioned work by Field and Bunney. The "wilderness" was the 'Grove Wilderness', which is shown, by land deeds, to have comprised Chalkhill, Spring Close, Roomes (planted with walnut trees), the Little Pightle (planted with plum trees) and Craddocks (planted with cherry trees). It formed a predominantly wooded belt of land along the southern border of the estate and constituted a fashionable appurtenance of a contemporary park. (In Aubrey's book it is said that Carshalton Park had a wilderness, too). In fact, the name was still being applied early in this century to "the area between the Water Tower and the front gate", according to an article in a 1973 issue of the school magazine *Philomena*.

Edward Carleton's five fish ponds are not now identifiable, but they were clearly all within the precincts of the mansion. It seems possible that the lake had been subdivided in some way to make 'pens' where catches of fish could be easily made when required for the kitchen. But old estate maps show small ponds also in other parts of the grounds.

Many new buildings have been put up since Carshalton House became a school, and the house that Edward Carleton built has had a wide variety of occupants since his time. But the mansion still remains very much what it was in the early 1700s, and its present grounds are very largely the fields and 'closes' which once surrounded The Old Farm. (One of those, called Coulsons or Coulsdons or Colstons, is mentioned in the Court Rolls in medieval times and still went with Carshalton House in the 19th century, though now the railway and Colston Avenue cut across it and houses have been built on it.) However, in the immediate vicinity of the house, such changes as have been made during the last three centuries have not altered its character essentially; its builder would still recognise it as his work, and to the modern eye it unmistakeably belongs to the Queen Anne period.

CHAPTER THREE

Life with the Carletons

By the middle of the 17th century there were a number of branches of the Carleton family in various parts of England, and more than one favoured Edward as a Christian name for its sons. However, Sister Pauline Stevens was able to find out, through the Mercers' Company, that the father of Edward Carleton of Carshalton House was another Edward, "late of Chertsey", who, after the usual seven years' apprenticeship, had been admitted to membership of the Company in 1631. Our Edward was, in due course, apprenticed to his father, and became a full member of the Company in 1662. In 1700 he took his own son, Arden, as an apprentice, and the latter was received into the Company in 1707. All this did not mean, though, that either Edward actually traded as a mercer. Membership of the City Companies had already largely become, as it is now, a status symbol; and the apprenticeships served were often purely nominal, acting merely as a means of passing on in the family a coveted social distinction. In fact, the Carshalton Edward Carleton was a tobacco merchant, and Arden became a partner in his father's business.

Some information about Edward Carleton's business interests is obtainable from a monograph on the Russian tobacco trade, written by Professor Jacob M. Price of Michigan University, published in 1961 by the American Philosophical Society, and brought to the notice of Sister Pauline Stevens by Dr. John Clarke of All Souls' College, Oxford. The Carleton firm imported its wares from Virginia and Maryland, had re-export outlets in Rotterdam and Riga, and also maintained trading relationships in Ireland, Sicily, the East Indies and Carolina. The printed State Papers for 1703 contain a petition, dated the 15th March, from Edward and Dudley Carleton, "merchants of London", which gives an illustration of trading hazards of the time. (This was, of course, before Arden had qualified to become his father's partner, and Sister Pauline Stevens's researches indicate that Dudley Carleton was Edward's twenty year younger brother.) The two men were the "owners and freighters" of the *Providence*, a ship of 300 tons, crewed by 18 men, armed with 16 guns, and bound for Maryland. In the assurance of being included in a convoy, this vessel had been made all ready for sailing, when "the embargo came", making half the crew liable to be transferred to "her Majesty's service". (This was the time when Marlborough was making his reputation in the war against the French and privateering on the high seas was rife.) The result of the government edict was that the whole crew deserted, "and, in spite of all endeavours, they *[the partners]* have not been able to make up their quota, and cannot do so before the convoy sails." They petitioned, nevertheless, that the *Providence* should be allowed to join the convoy and receive "protection for her crew".

Like other merchants of his time Edward Carleton would participate in any commercial enterprise which seemed likely to prove profitable, even though it was in a previously unexplored field. So it is not surprising to find that he was one of the first to respond to an appeal for subscriptions made by the Russian Tobacco Company, which had been formed in 1698 to exploit a monopoly granted by Peter the Great (for a substantial financial inducement) in respect of the import of tobacco into Russia. (It is of incidental interest that another of the seven original subscribers of £2,000 each to "The Tobacco Adventure in Russia" was Sir William Scawen, the very rich merchant-financier and ex-Governor of the Bank of England, who lived in the Carshalton Park mansion.) But, in spite of the monopoly granted by the Tsar, the English tobacco merchants found it difficult to oust the long-established Baltic suppliers from the Russian market, and this 'Adventure' was not a lasting success. Nevertheless the going cold of this one iron in Edward Carleton's trading fire could hardly have caused the failure which eventually overtook the thriving business he had built up over the years. In fact, there is no hint anywhere of the reason for that. All that the surviving documents show is that, between 1709 and 1711, Edward and Arden Carleton gave to the Commissioners of Customs bonds (backed by sureties) to a total of some £16,000 for unpaid tobacco duty which still remained unpaid in 1713; and, by then, the partnership owed a further £15,000 to trade creditors.

In these days of dizzily accelerating currency debasement such sums may not sound unduly large; but, at the time, they would have paid for ten mansions like Carshalton House, so, half a million pounds in modern money would be a very conservative estimate of the Carletons' total liabilities. The giving of bonds for the payment of tobacco duty was a legally permissible option which importers had until 1787, when bonded warehouses were introduced, but eighteen months was the maximum period for which settlement might be delayed, and discounts were given for earlier payment. In the circumstances, the Commissioners of Customs showed surprising forbearance in not taking legal action on the unredeemed bonds until 1713.

What happened after that is detailed in the next chapter; but one result of the enforcement proceedings was that an official inventory of the contents of Carshalton House had to be made. And that document (a copy of which is in the Surrey Record Office at Kingston) is an invaluable source of information about what the mansion was like when it was first built. The inventory is also of considerable general interest because it lists in the minutest detail all the accessories to domestic life in a wealthy Englishman's home in the early part of the 18th century. (It even names materials and objects which are not to be found in the 'O.E.D.'.) Taking it, however, merely as evidence of the lay-out of Carshalton House in Edward Carleton's time, it presents straightaway a surprise and a puzzle. On the ground floor the inventory mentions only a "great Stair case and Hall", four "Parlours" (what a modern estate agent would call 'reception rooms'), a kitchen and a "back kitchen", whereas the modern mansion shows no ground

16

floor kitchen but seven main rooms. This apparent increase in accommodation was, I believe, achieved by removing a "great staircase" from a centrally situated entrance hall and dividing the latter into two rooms; and, in Chapters 6 and 7, I detail the circumstances which have led me to this conclusion.

The Carleton great staircase and hall were certainly furnished on a scale which it would be difficult to reproduce within the comparatively modest dimensions of the mansion's present-day entrance hall. In the early 18th century the Hall was clearly the focal point of the building; it even held a "Fether bedd & bolster, a rugg, two Blanketts & a Bedstead" — which would seem to indicate that a servant was required to be available here throughout the night, but might sleep if circumstances permitted. The other furnishings of the Carleton hall were, however, of a quite different and not at all a humble character. The inventory lists "19 rown (?round) Chairs with Ovall Backs, 4 ovall Tables, an eight Day Clock & Case, two Bird Cages, 47 pictures and a Glass Lanthorn" (the latter being evidently an enclosed candelabra suspended from the ceiling, and, in the Fellowes' inventory 8 years later, described as having "Lines and Pullies"). There was also a fireplace — something which the present hall cannot show and for which it could hardly provide a suitable site. It seems probable that when the Carletons entertained on a large scale, the festivities centred on the great hall; and it is surely not being over-imaginative to picture it as the scene of grand balls, with the local gentry, during the intervals between dances, disposing themselves on the 19 rown chairs (and others from the Parlours) while consuming refreshments served from the four Ovall tables.

Somewhere near the foot of the great staircase were two "Closetts", which held the means of providing entertainment of a different kind, namely, "a fishing Cane, playing Tables & Men, Boxes & Dice". But these closets were capacious enough to serve also as a depository for anything not wanted for the time being, for they also housed "a Carpett, a Matt, a Ladder, four Wooden Stands, a hand Tea table, Six Cups and Saucers, some China, Earthen Ware & Glasses", together with "Boxes & Basketts & Lumber". In effect, the Carletons had here what some families call a 'glory hole'.

It is not possible, from the contents of the four 'Parlours' to deduce their precise respective uses in modern terms. But the one called "The Comon Parlour" was probably a room in which meals were served; it was, at any rate, handily adjacent to the kitchen (see the plan on page 43). It contained "3 Ovall Tables, 12 Cane Chairs with 12 Cushions, and a Stuff Elbow Chair", but it must be said that the "Cane Couche & Cushions", which were also in it, would not normally be found in a present-day dining room. The other equipment of the "Comon Parlour", apart from window curtains, was "4 Pictures, 2 Sconces [i.e. *candle holders*], 6 China Canisters, and a Stove Grate & Fender". The room also had a Closet in which there were "a Desk & Table" and a second fireplace. At the time it was usual for the rooms of the gentry to have free-standing fire baskets on tiled hearths, so what was termed in the Carleton inventory a "hearth" or a "grate" was, legally, a chattel and not part of the structure.

The other three "Parlours" can be identified as the rooms which occupy the east front of the mansion. The middle one, with its "20 Silk Chairs, 3 Stools with Cases [i.e. *covers*] of Green Sarge, 2 Walnutt Tree Card Tables" and a "Tea Table" was clearly intended for the reception of 'company' in considerable numbers. It

17

was, in fact, the show piece of the ground floor, its contents being valued in the inventory at £44. 4s. – nearly twice as much in money's worth as any other Parlour contained. It alone had "a matt on the Flour"; but, undoubtedly, the most valuable objects in it and its "Closett" were the ornaments and china. These comprised "6 Pictures, 20 Prints, 3 large China Jarrs, 4 Canisters, 2 large Punch Bowls, 4 large Dishes, a Barbers Bason, 2 small Punch Bowles & Covers, 9 Sugar Dishes & Covers, 4 Japan Dishes & Covers, 2 Plates, 7 Basions [sic] & 34 Pieces of small China Ware". Oriental porcelain in the early 18th century was highly fashionable and the pieces in this collection would undoubtedly have been expensive acquisitions. The room where they were displayed was the one, now called the "Oak Room", which Sir John Fellowes later embellished with a magnificent carved wooden chimney-piece bearing his arms. (He also had – probably on view in this room – a set of blue and white china, made in China and decorated with his arms, some pieces of which were still in existence when, in 1910, the Rev. E. H. Fellowes (who himself owned several of them) wrote "The Family and Descendants of William Fellowes of Eggesford".)

The Carleton inventory shows that, adjoining the principal drawing-room, was "the painted Parlour", and this is identifiable as the room next to the Oak Room on the north side, the walls of which are still covered with 18th century paintings. In Edward Carleton's time it contained "a Marble Table, a Double Settee, 3 Elbow Chairs, 5 Stools, 3 China Jarrs, a Punch, 12 Basins, 5 Plates, 2 Sugar Dishes & Covers and a Beaker & Saucer" – an ensemble designed for use in circumstances not now easy to imagine. But this must have been regarded as a rather special Parlour, because it had "two Locks and bolts to the two Doors". Perhaps it was the private sanctum of the master of the house?

The room on the other side of the Oak Room had, in 1713, seats for only a small number of people, and it seems to have been reserved for games players. At any rate it was furnished with "2 Card Tables, 7 Elbow Chairs, 5 Stools of Silk, a Couche & three Cushions, an Ovall Table, a tea Table, 7 Pictures, a China Jarr, 2 beakers, 3 large China Dishes, 2 Plates, 6 Basins, a Sugar Dish and 18 Pieces of China Ware".

This Parlour, like all the others except the 'Painted' one, had a "Closett" with its own fireplace additional to the one which served the main room. These closets seem to have been intended to enable private conversations to be carried on while the Parlour itself was in general use; and such apparently unsocial behaviour must have been accepted, in the 18th century, as no breach of good manners. One thing can be said with some confidence: nobody retired to a closet for a quiet read. As Sister Pauline Stevens pointed out – something I had failed to notice myself – not a single book is mentioned anywhere in the Carleton inventory; and there is no musical instrument listed either.

The household may have been ill supplied with food for the mind (though it did have numerous pictures on the walls), but it was well equipped with everything required for the nourishment of the body. The inventory shows the kitchen and back kitchen to have lacked nothing contemporaneously used in the preparation and service of eatables. Well over a hundred items are particularised, starting with the kitchen range, its spits and fireirons, and ending with "a Pail & Lumber". The cooking utensils included "an Iron Dripping Pan & Frame, 3 Bell Mettle & one brass pott & 3 Covers, 2 Bell Mettle Skellets, 4 Brass Skellets,

3 Sauce Pans, 4 Stew Pans, 3 Kettles, a ffish Kettle, Cover & Plate, a Gridiron, 2 Frying Pans and 2 Iron Peeles" (*baker's shovels*). The cook had also the use of "a Jack and wigh (? *weight*) with a Multiplying Wheele (*a gear wheel*), a Coffee Mill, a Chopping Knife, a grater, a Spice Box, a Salt box, 2 Morters & a Pestle, 2 Cullenders, 5 Sieves, a Pair of Scales and two Tin Pasty Pans". For the serving and consumption of food and drink the Carletons had "25 Pewter Dishes, 4 Mazarine (a deep dish), 80 plates, 2 Coffee Drinking Potts, a Chocolate Pott, 2 Chaffing (*sic*) Dishes" and "knives & Glasses". But there were only 2 forks — used apparently for cooking — and no spoons at all. Had some of the cutlery been put out of the reach of the inventory takers because it was silver? Finally came equipment for maintaining table linen in good condition, namely, "5 Box Irons & Heaters", together with "a Napkin Press". The kitchen and back kitchen were indeed places where there was plenty to keep the staff occupied, but little encouragement to sit in idleness — only "2 Formes and 3 Stools". However, in those days workers would not have regarded it as unreasonable that they should be expected to work hard. And they would probably have accepted without complaining, too, the unspecified "earthen, tin and Wooden ware" which seems to have been what they had to eat and drink from.

In the inventory, the "Dary" comes next after the back kitchen, and it is probable that both were buildings outside the main block of the house. The back kitchen was almost certainly the room which is still traceable as a former westward addition to the old ground floor kitchen. Underneath it is what is called the 'Tudor' cellar, which similarly extends beyond the rectangle of the basement. There are chalk blocks in the walls of this cellar, and, at its western end, it appears to have been blocked off from a continuation. Was this part of the foundations of The Old Farm? Sister Pauline Stevens has studied its oddities very closely but is still undecided as to their significance — although it does seem pretty certain that the 'Tudor' cellar is older than the rest of the basement. The puzzle it presents might be solved if it was known what lies beyond its west wall. In any case, putting a room on top of it created an excrescence which spoiled the symmetry so characteristic of 'Queen Anne' architecture; and there must have been some good reason for that.

Edward Carleton's dairy contained a churn, 2 cheese tubs, 6 pails, 3 lead pans, a two quart pot, a cheese press and "some earthen Pans and Wood Ware." He had his own cows, so these utensils would have been in daily use.

The main door of the front kitchen opened on to a passage from which stairs went down into the basement. Here there was a quantity of Lumber, and also "a Dough Tub, a Flower Tub, 2 Chopping Blocks, a Chopping Knife and a Bolting Mill" which appear to have overflowed from the kitchen. In fact, the dough and floor tubs suggest that the household's daily bread was actually prepared downstairs — and possibly baked there too (it certainly was in the 19th century). The basement also contained a Candle Chest, and, though nothing is said about its contents, it must have been kept well filled, because the mansion was entirely dependent on candles for its lighting. But undoubtedly the most important contents of the cellars were the 4 barrels, 3 kilderkins and 8 hogs heads, which also had to be kept well filled in an 18th century gentleman's residence. And the "bottle rack and 2 Grose of Bottles" would surely not have been preserved and listed if they had not contained Edward Carleton's wine.

The passage which lay between the kitchen and the 'Comon Parlour' contained 2 tables, a carpet, some chairs and an unspecified number of pictures. It led to the usual domestic offices of the time, housed in a separate block. First came the brewhouse, in which were installed all the vats, tubs, troughs, pumps and piping for the production of what would have been the everyday tipple of both family and staff. In a "Room over the Brewhouse" there was "a bedstead & old Curtains *[evidently a pensioned-off four-poster]*, a Fether bedd, a bowlster, a Quilt and two Old Chairs". This was quite sumptuous bedroom furniture for a servant, and he would have had, in addition, the fumes of the brewery to help keep him happy.

After the Brewhouse came the Washhouse, containing 4 tubs, a horse, more piping, and 3 forms. Awaiting treatment here was some "Foul Linnen", separately listed. But much the greater part of the "Linnen" was apparently clean. Under that heading came 4 pairs of calico sheets, 36 towels, 30 pillowcases, 35 table cloths, 65 napkins, 5 bed ticks and 4 dozen pillows.

The domestic offices outside the main building probably formed two sides of a square, because, after the Washhouse, the inventory mentions a "back Yard" in which there were "2 leaden Cisterns, 2 Pumps, 2 Tubbs, a Water Cart & Barrell *[no doubt principally for use in case of fire]*, a Grindstone, 3 Ladders and a parcel of Wood". (There is no evidence that anything else was used for fuel in the house.)

Edward Carleton's transport was kept in "the Fore Yard", and it was probably over the stables here that the "Coachman & Boys Roome" was located. It contained only "2 Fether bedds and Bowlsters, 2 Ruggs, 2 Blanketts and 4 Sheets" to keep the coachman and his assistant warm. During the day they had to look after a coach, a chariot (a light carriage) and seven horses; but some of the horses may have worked in the fields because the Carshalton House land was being farmed by the owner of the mansion. This is made clear by the presence in the Foreyard of "4 Cows, 12 Hogs, a Waggon, a Plough & 2 Harrows, 80 Load of Hay, and about 30 Load of Dung". Fifty-five acres of land in all were under cultivation, barley accounting for 30, wheat for 12 (2 of which were "spoiled"), beans for 7 and peas for 6 (a good part of those last two crops would probably have been dried for winter consumption).

The estimated yields of the farm produce do not suggest that there would have been much surplus after domestic needs had been met. At the time — and for long afterwards — it was customary for men of wealth to grow their own food as much as possible; and Edward Carleton was not failing to live up to the social pretensions of his new house by having a smelly farmyard behind it. His garden lay on the other side of the mansion to the south and east; and, judging from what the inventory takers found in it, it was well maintained and must have been a highly regarded amenity. With a total value of £11. 5s. (the same figure that was placed on the contents of the cellars) there are listed "in the garden": "4 Stone rollers, a parcell of Potts & 2 leaden Potts, all the Garden Tools, 2 Water Potts, 1 Wheel Barrow, 3 Frames with 8 Glass lights, 12 Bell Glasses, 2 Seats, 2 Boats and 8 Chairs in the Summer House." It appears from these last items that the lake was already treated as an ornamental feature of the grounds, to be enjoyed both on its surface and from a comfortable viewing point. But it is impossible to be sure now where exactly the Carleton summer house was or what the shape of the lake was at this time. (In the late nineteenth century there was a summer house by the mock bridge at the north end of the lake, but this is not likely to have been nearly 200 years old.)

It seems that the view from the best bedroom did not embrace the garden, because what the inventory takers described as "Madam Carleton's room" on the first floor is identifiable as the middle bedroom on the north side. (The corresponding south-facing bedroom is considerably smaller — which could have been a consequence of space having to be found for the head of a grand staircase rising from a central hall.) It is understandable that Edward Carleton's name was not attached to any bedroom in the inventory, because he is officially reported to have absconded when his bankruptcy was imminent. But the best bedroom in Carshalton House was not to remain even his wife's for much longer. The Parish Registers record the burial of Mary Carleton on the 12th June 1713, shortly after the inventory was made.

In life she had slept in "a wrought *[i.e. needleworked]* bed lined with Striped Silk". (The beds of the well-off at that time were, of course, 'four-posters' with curtains which could be drawn all round.) The bed furniture comprised "a Feather bed and bolster, two Blanketts, two holland Quilts, a calico Quilt and a Callico Counterpaine". There were also in Madam Carleton's room "a wainscott *[i.e. oak]* Chest of Drawers, five silk Chairs, four Stools with Cases *[fabric covers]* ", three other stools, two tables and seven China Basins; while, on the walls, there hung "two Pictures, a Print and two Pieces of Tapestry". This room was regarded as important enough to have "4 Locks and keys to the Doors" — a number which suggests that there was a closet in the room, although it is not mentioned by the inventory takers. Four of the other five first floor rooms which were furnished with beds are specified to have had either a "Closett" or a "Dressing Roome" adjoining, and it seems unlikely that the mistress of the house would have been without that amenity. (This was the 'Capital Bed Room' when the property was sold in 1839 and it then had "Dressing and Water Closets adjoining".) The four bedrooms in question are, in the inventory, named after the material used for the bed hangings; so there was another "wrought Roome", a "Chints Roome", a "redd Damask Room" and a "blue Damask Room". It seems that Madam Carleton had stuck to the by now old-fashioned furniture of her early married life, because the four bedrooms with closets were furnished in a different — and more costly — style than hers. The other "wrought" room, for instance, had eight elbow chairs, ten stools, "an Indian Cabinet, two Black Tables & Covers, two Peer Glasses of Steel, a Dressing Glass, a large Jarr and 17 other pieces of China Ware". The estimated value of these articles, together with the bed, bedding and window curtains, was £73. 2s, whereas £40. 16s. (itself a high figure) covered the contents of Madam Carleton's bedroom. But the second "wrought" room must have been far outdone in splendour by the Red Damask room. That accounted for £100. 2s. in the inventory totals — more than twice the value given to the furnishings of any of the Parlours. The seating accommodation in the "redd Room" included, besides 4 Stools with Cases and 8 Damask Chairs, "a Damask easy Chair", which was in the very height of fashion, for the O.E.D.'s first reported use of the term 'easy chair' is dated only six years earlier, in 1707. In addition to its red damask furnishings and silk window curtains, this bedroom and its "Closetts" also held "an Indian Skreen, two Japan Tables and Covers, a Chimney Glass, a Dressing Glass, two tables, four Pieces of Tapestry Hangings, and — a rather deflating but no doubt necessary anti-climax — "four Brooms and a Brush".

The blue Damask Room ranked lowest among the principal bedrooms, accounting for only £39. 9s. in the inventory values. It held "eight Chairs of the same *[i.e. blue damask]* with Cases and one Piece of Tapestry", but, apart from that, nothing exotic except an "Inleid Table". The "Chints Room", with 2 tables, 5 elbow cane chairs and 5 crimson damask cushions, 5 silk stools & cases, one damask easy chair and "one Walnutt Tree Chest of Drawers" sounds to have been much more luxuriously furnished, but the total value of its contents was only £40.

The accessories in "the furthest Roome on the Stairs" (probably the bedroom over the Painted Parlour) figured in the inventory at a mere £10. 5s. and were evidently of an inferior quality, for, with 6 chairs, 2 stools, a table, a quilted basket, a large trunk and 2 pieces of tapestry – in addition to its "Bedstead and Scarlet and blew worsted Damask Furniture" – the room was by no means inadequately equipped. (And it must be said that its contents were worth almost as much as those of the common parlour.)

The remaining "Roome at the End of the Gallery" on the first floor is rather a puzzle because, although it was quite well furnished, it had no fireplace furniture, and no bed either; only a "Couch and Pillow". Its "three Suits of Yellow Silke Window Curtains", six silk stools, chest of drawers, black table, 2 stands, looking glass, "three Mapps, seventy Prints, three Glasses with Covers, sweetmeat Frame, thirty six Pieces of China Ware and two Locks & Keys" were, however, worth in all £13, if the inventory takers had correctly valued the prints and china. Some of the contents of this room indicate that it was treated as a kind of art gallery; and it is perhaps more than a chance coincidence that, in 1839, when the mansion was up for sale, one room on the first floor was described as being "decorated with well-selected prints".

All the rooms on the first floor opened off a long gallery and even this had its quota of expensive furnishings. Disposed along it were 4 carpets, 2 Spanish Tables, 12 Turkey Work Chairs, an elbow Chair, a Couch, 3 Cushions, a Press, a Stand, some Shelves and a Basin; while, on the walls, there hung 28 pictures, some prints and a hatchment (armorial bearings).

The known family of Edward Carleton in 1713 could not have required six bedrooms for its accommodation, but, in his day, hospitality on a very generous scale was extended freely to both relatives and friends who lived at a distance. Even so, there seems to have been an extravagant number of chairs and stools in these bedrooms. They seem almost to have been sumptuously furnished so that they could be used by their occupants for the reception of visitors. In this connection a discovery made by Sister Pauline Stevens may have significance. On two of the bedroom doors she found traces of an ingenious fitment which, by means of a cord running from it to the bed, once allowed the occupant, without getting up, to unbolt the door when ready to be seen. And it is possible that all the first floor bedrooms were originally fitted with this device. Their contents were certainly eminently suited to public display (the value put on them was more than twice that put on the contents of the ground floor rooms). But who could have been keeping such state in Carshalton House? It was a country residence, not, so far as is known, a fashionable resort of polite society. As with much else in the Carleton story, there is an enigma here. One thing stands out clearly, though: this 18th century tobacco merchant had not stinted money on his home – which, perhaps, helps to explain his eventual financial downfall.

His domestic staff seems to have been mainly accommodated on the second floor of the mansion, so, not surprisingly, the bedrooms there were much more modestly furnished. Nevertheless, except for one which contained only drugget hangings and some shelves, they all had four-poster beds. The "Cook's Roome" had "purple Clothe & ffurniture" to the "Beadsted", though the only other furniture in it was "two Truncks, a Box, a Chair, a Stool, a Glass and a Cushion". However, the cook no doubt slept comfortably on her feather bed and bolster, covered with "a Holland Quilt, three Blanketts, a Calico Quilt, a rugg and a Counterpain".

Two of the bedrooms on this floor had contents more valuable than those of "the furthest Roome on the Stairs" below. But "Madam Mary's Room & Closet" − which, presumably, was where the daughter born to Edward and Mary Carleton in 1691 slept − accounted for only £7. 10s. in the inventory totals. She was provided only with a bed with drugget hangings, "an Ovall Table, two chairs and a stool". But, like the Cook, she should, at least have been able to sleep warmly on her feather bed with its five blankets and a quilt. Next to her room was "Madam Skinner's Room", the contents of which were worth only £6. 10s., although, with two tables, three chairs, two stools and a glass, she had more furniture than Madam Mary. The maiden name of Edward Carleton's second wife had been Skinner, so his younger daughter's neighbour on the top floor was probably a "poor relation". But, judging from Mary's room, if Madam Skinner had been a daughter of the house she would have been little better accommodated at night. It does indeed seem that, in his allocation of bedrooms, Edward Carleton was more concerned with impressing visitors than with how his family was faring. But it is unlikely that the spartan conditions in her room had anything to do with Mary's death two years later. A number of the Carleton children were short-lived; one died soon after birth, another at 15, and a third in his twenties. It is not known how long Theodosia (who married in 1710) and Arden lived.

Edward Carleton's chattels in Carshalton House were advertised for sale together with the mansion, and, after coming into the possession of Dr. John Radcliffe, they passed, as a result of the sale, to Sir John Fellowes. And the latter still had a large number of them when an inventory of his furnishings came to be made in 1720. (It was Sister Pauline Stevens who first noticed the unmistakeable correspondences in the two lists.)

How the Carleton estate came into Fellowes's possession is related in the next chapter. This one should end with an account of Edward Carleton's subsequent career, but, unfortunately, I have been unable to discover anything about it. As already mentioned, he and Arden absconded when ruin was inevitable. Arden was made bankrupt and then disappears entirely from the records. But the *London Gazette* for the 27th November 1714 announced that Edward Carleton had surrendered to be examined by a 'Commission of Bankrupt' which had been set up in his case, and that he would attend "at the Two Fighting Cocks in the Mint" on the 8th December "in order to finish his Examination". The next mention I found of him after that was a report in the *Gentleman's Magazine* that, on the 5th November 1732, "Mr. Carleton died at Newington Green, formerly an eminent Merchant". The parish registers show that he was buried in Carshalton on the 11th November, so he must have still regarded our village as his true home. It is evident also that his misfortunes had not shortened his life; in 1732 he cannot have been far away − one side or the other − from his 90th birthday.

Although we really know comparatively little about the man who was responsible for the building of Carshalton House, he could have asked for nothing better by which to be remembered than that creation. And, provided that fine buildings of the past continue to be a treasured part of our national heritage, it is likely to remain for a long time yet as a kind of memorial to Edward Carleton. There are few merchants of his time who have left anything comparable to commemorate them. (It is possible, too, that pieces of the splendid furniture which once filled his rooms still survive — anonymously — in some modern great house or museum.)

CHAPTER FOUR

Dr. John Radcliffe

Early in 1714 Carshalton House, in circumstances which will be detailed later in this chapter, became the residence of Dr. John Radcliffe, a well-known physician of his time, who was frequently consulted by royalty. His high professional reputation was, however, somewhat blemished by an outspokenness which often became rudeness. Even monarchs were not exempt from the brusqueness of his tongue; when treating William III's swollen ankles, he is reported to have said "Why, truly, I would not have Your Majesty's two legs for your three kingdoms" — a remark which did not go down well with his royal patient.

Nevertheless, Dr. Radcliffe remained in high esteem as a medico, and when Queen Anne became seriously ill in July 1714, he was sent for. But, either objecting to the informality of the summons or pleading his own ill health (accounts vary) he declined to go to London. In consequence, after the Queen's death on the 1st August, there was very strong feeling against Dr. Radcliffe in the Tory party which stood to lose power by the Hanoverian succession. Mob passions ran high in the capital, and the doctor wrote to a friend that he would not be leaving Carshalton "because I have received several letters that threaten me with being pulled in pieces if ever I come to London".

Exactly three months after his Queen had died, Dr. Radcliffe followed her to the grave, the cause of death in both cases being given as apoplexy — what we should call a stroke. It was ironical that the doctor should have come to Carshalton to die. When Carshalton House was for sale in 1888, the auctioneers asserted — on what authority is not known — that "Carshalton, from its salubrious and delightful situation was styled by Dr. Radcliffe, the celebrated physician who resided there in the reign of Queen Anne, 'the Montpelier of England' ". How anyone could have seen a resemblance between that town in the south of France and our Surrey village is beyond my understanding, but there is no doubt that Carshalton did have a high reputation for its salubrious and delightful situation.

Dr. Radcliffe's own reputation suffered a marked decline after his death. Manning and Bray, in their monumental history of Surrey, wrote of him that "He amassed great wealth and was prompted by his vanity to give it to the University of Oxford to found a Library which was to be called by his name, and to build an observatory." The Rotunda in Oxford was built with the doctor's legacy to house the 'Radcliffe Library' but that, in 1861, was merged in the New Museum and the

An engraving made from a portrait by Sir Godfrey Kneller.

JOHANNES RADCLIFFE MD.

Obijt 1º. Nov. MDCCXIV.

Ætat. 65

G. Kneller Baron. Pinx.t 1710.

P. Fourdrinier Sculp. 1747.

26

Rotunda (now called the Radcliffe Camera) became part of the Bodleian Library. The Radcliffe Observatory and the Radcliffe Infirmary also survive to commemorate his name – or perhaps his vanity.

So far as Carshalton was concerned Dr. Radcliffe continued to be a great name in its history. In a 1922 issue of the school magazine of *St. Philomena's* one of the senior girls gave what purported to be the reminiscences of an ancient frog living in Carshalton House's lake; and, by his account, the original house was built by Dr. Radcliffe – a piece of misinformation which had been passed on to him by some sparrows who, I suspect, obtained it from Manning and Bray. But I have not been able to trace the source of all the stories about the doctor which are attributed, in the article, to various animals inhabiting the grounds. Those have him talking about the mansion to Pope and Harley, quarrelling with Swift, who turns on his heel muttering "insolent puppy", and embarking with an actor on a "mercantile venture" which loses the doctor £3,000. According to the *Dictionary of National Biography* Dr. Radcliffe actually lost £5,000 in 1692 owing to the capture by the French of a ship in which he had invested money on the advice of the actor Betterton. The only conversation with Pope mentioned by this authority is the doctor's advice to him at the age of 17 to study less and ride more – which is said to have helped the young poet regain his health. As for Swift, all the 'D.N.B.' has to say is that, in 1711, Dr. Radcliffe treated him for dizziness, and later that year Swift wrote to Stella that "that puppy Radcliffe" was responsible for the neglect of Harley's wound.

Belief in the authenticity of the happenings reported by the ancient frog is not helped by his averring that Dr. Radcliffe lived in Carshalton House for several years prior to his death. But this Batrachian Patriarch (as he is termed in the article) should not be too harshly criticised; he was only following the example of many local historians – and some national ones – by using his imagination and relying on unreliable information.

And now for the story (this time, a true one) of how Dr. Radcliffe came to live in Carshalton House. It starts with the financial troubles of the Carletons. When they failed to pay the tobacco duty in respect of which they had given bonds, the Commissioners of Customs were able to resort to a legal remedy available only to the Crown and thus get ahead of the trade creditors in laying hands on Edward Carleton's assets. They obtained, in the Exchequer Court, what were called 'writs of extent', and, on the strength of those, a Sheriff's order was made in September 1713 for the seizure and sale of the Carshalton estate. It was in the course of these proceedings that the inventory was drawn up which has given us so much information about the mansion in its early days. The Commissioners of Customs, however, were not concerned with posterity but with the immediate value to them of the property seized. So their next step was to put a notice in February 1714 issues of the *London Gazette* inviting tenders for the Carleton mansion, land and furniture as one lot. The best bid received, from Dr. Radcliffe, was one of £7,163 (which included the inventory total for the furnishings and £3,000 "for the House, Stables & a Garden and spring or Grove"); and, in April, the total purchase price having been paid, possession of the estate was given to the doctor. The Customs Commissioners were, however, in a difficulty over giving him a legal title to the premises. The Attorney General, when consulted, advised that Edward Carleton should be required to "join with the Crowne in the Sale", and, if he declined, the writs of extent should be enforced by imprisonment. In case that failed to "bring him to a Complyance", the Attorney General's opinion was that a title could be conferred on Dr. Radcliffe under the Queen's seal. (The monarch was, in legal theory, the ultimate owner of all the country's land.)

As Mr. Carleton had put himself safely out of reach of the law, there was no alternative but to obtain a royal warrant of grant, and on the 26th May a letter went from Custom House to the Treasury requesting that the necessary document be prepared, sealed and signed. The leisurely pace at which civil servants work is not just a modern phenomenon. Dr. Radcliffe's warrant was not ready for Queen Anne's signature until the 28th July. In the meantime she had been taken seriously ill, and on the 1st August long life was being wished to her successor, George I. The grant of the Carshalton property had not been signed by the late Queen, and, as the law then stood, this was business personal to the monarch and did not devolve automatically on the new King. However, nobody seems to have been seriously worried about the situation at the time, for, on the 12th October, a letter was sent by the Customs authority to the Treasury, referring to the preparation of "a title for Dr. Radcliffe" as if it was just a routine procedure.

But apparently nothing more was done before the doctor himself died on the 1st November. His executors may not have been aware that anything was amiss with the title to the Carleton estate; at any rate, they gave notice in December issues of the *London Gazette* that it was for sale to "the best Bidder". The winner in this competition was John Fellowes, about whom all that need be said at this stage is that he was a very wealthy London merchant-financier. What he offered for the Carshalton property does not appear from the surviving documents. The next in date of those is a letter of the 26th March 1715 from the Attorney General concerning a warrant to pass Dr. Radcliffe's title to his executors. This is minuted by the Treasury: "My Lords have directed the Com^{rs} of the Customs to put up this estate to ye best bidder" — which meant that the sale to Dr. Radcliffe was to be treated as a nullity because the warrant sanctioning it had not been signed by Queen Anne. The Treasury could be slack in some ways, but it was a stickler in others.

The property must have been advertised for sale again, because, in a conveyance which was later drawn up it is stated: "Whereas public notice was given of the sale to the best bidder in the London Gazette pursuant to an order made 14th March 1714 (*1715 N.S.*) and no one else appeared to bid for the estate but John Fellowes . . .". (Other potential purchasers would, no doubt, have been put off by uncertainties over the title.) However, Fellowes' bid — again of a sum not mentioned in the records — did not finally settle the matter. The Treasury had a number of other interested parties to deal with. There was first of all a reaction from the 'Commission of Bankrupt', which had been set up on the 16th July 1714, presumably on the petition of the trade creditors of Edward Carleton. The Commission had appointed Sir William Scawen of Carshalton Park to be its trustee, and he now wrote to the Treasury suggesting that the estate should be granted to him for the benefit of the creditors, in return for his undertaking to pay £7,163 to the executors and also to "satisfy [them] for any improvements made". That latter offer was an attempt to meet another complication which had arisen: Dr. Radcliffe's executors were claiming that he had "made severall alterations and improvements on the premises which, with the repairs and the surveying the estate, amounted to above 900[1]". The executors were evidently not impressed by Sir William Scawen's offer, for they wrote to the Treasury asking that "the lease may be perfected".

The upshot of all this was a request by the Treasury for a report on the whole matter from the Commissioners of Customs. Having received that in due course, the Treasury then asked the Attorney General and the Solicitor General for a report on the report. All this took time and not until the 10th September did the Treasury receive the opinion of the Law Officers of the Crown. It then acted with amazing swiftness and on the 12th September once more ordered that the Carleton estate should be put up for sale again. There followed promptly an urgent petition jointly from the executors and John Fellowes that they be heard before their Lordships (of the Treasury) "by their Councell upon the validity of the said Doct[r] Radcliffe's contract and agreement". At the very least, they contended, the money he had spent on the estate should be reimbursed with interest. (On a straightforward re-sale, the purchaser would, of course, have obtained the benefit of any improvements made by Dr. Radcliffe and no compensation would have been due to his executors if he had never been the legal owner of the premises.)

The executors' petition was minuted by the Treasury; "The sale suspended; lr̃e *[letter]* writ.", and, on the 15th November 1715, all parties concerned came before four Lords of the Treasury for a full hearing of the case. The Attorney General, the Solicitor General and the Commissioners of Customs attended in person; the executors and the creditors were each represented by counsel; Fellowes was present but had no separate legal representation; and the principal guarantor of the Carleton bonds was also there. The minutes of the hearing do not always make it quite clear what exactly was being argued, and they were probably made by someone not experienced in taking a note of judicial proceedings. But it seems that the Attorney and Solicitor General had mentioned an additional payment of £500 to the Crown, since counsel for the executors, referring to their report, enquired indignantly: "Shall £500 violate all rules of justice and honour?"; and he went on to say: "If this were a case between man and man there could be no dispute." Counsel for the creditors, however, did not agree. He suggested that "what was laid out by the Dor *[Dr.]*, was no advantage, but in some cases worse for the estate". But his most serious assertion was that the original sale had not been "a fair bidding, for the Dor. had declared 'let others bid what they would, he would have it' " – an obvious hint at corruption somewhere. "Where an officer is to make a contract for the Crown and it shall appear to be disadvantageous before it is executed, it is not obligatory", argued counsel for the creditors.

Mr. Watkinson, the principal guarantor of the Carleton bonds was, apparently, not considered to have much to argue about after he had admitted that he did not bid for the property when it was advertised for sale. The Attorney and the Solicitor General wound up the debate by saying that they thought "the King is not bound to make the grant. However, if the estate is put to sale again, the accounting for interest on the money deposited *[the purchase price paid by Dr. Radcliffe]* and charges *[the money spent on the estate by him]* will leave the Crown no gainer". It did not seem to occur to the Law Officers that the Crown could not fairly expect to be a gainer by the Treasury's default.

The Treasury minute of the final decision reads as follows: "My Lords, on considering this case, are of opinion that, as to ye suretys and cred[rs] of Mr. Carlton, they having had due notice when this estate was offered for sale, and none appearing to bid more, have no reason to complain, and therefore my Lords can have no consideraćon for them, but their Lo[ps] *[Lordships]* think with Mr. Attor *[Attorney General]*, and Mr. Soll[r] *[Solicitor General]* that this bargain was not obligatory upon the Crown in strictness of law. Nevertheless, for ye hono[r] of the Crown, and in justice to the proceedings, my Lords, instead of setting the estate to sale again, will move the King to accept the 500 1. offered and to grant the Privy Seal immediately, to w[ch] Mr. Fellows (being first cal[d] in againe) agreed to; desiring that in regard to this 500 1. more bonds may be assigned to protect the estate." (Carleton bonds to the value of £7,163 had been transferred to Dr. Radcliffe as a sort of insurance against possible future claims.)

It is not clear from the record whether John Fellowes made his offer of an extra £500 before the Law Officers of the Crown had mentioned it in their report, or whether he had responded to a suggestion made by them, or whether, indeed, that had been his bid when the premises were advertised for sale in March. Anyway, the Crown turned out to be the gainer in the end. Nevertheless, Fellowes's agreement to pay roughly another 7% on the original purchase price indicates that he considered he was still getting a reasonable bargain. And what he had contracted to pay the executors was presumably more than they would have obtained from repayment of the £7,163, plus compensation for money spent on the estate, plus interest on both sums. It does rather look, then, as if the price Dr. Radcliffe paid was an under-valuation, even if no corruption was involved.

It is a pity that no record seems to have survived of what work on the estate the doctor had done during the few months he lived in Carshalton; but the alleged 'improvements' were not necessarily made to the mansion; they could have been carried out on the other properties which went with it.

The Treasury does not appear to have learned anything from what had happened to the warrant giving title to Dr. Radcliffe, for not until the 20th January 1716 was George I's signature appended to the Patent granting the Carleton estate to John Fellowes. Fortunately, the King turned out to be a better life risk than the late Queen.

In the meantime, the "suretys" to the Carleton bonds had made a last desperate petition to the Treasury to be heard by counsel, but this was minuted: "My Lords think they cannot hear this matter over again." Just as the creditors had more chance of getting something back if the Carleton estate fetched a higher price at a second sale, so, too, the potential liability of the sureties would have been correspondingly reduced. The latter had to remain disappointed, but Sir William Scawen, that wily old business tycoon, did eventually manage to salvage something for the creditors – and for himself. Sir John Fellowes found that his troubles with the Carshalton property were not yet over. The circumstances of the sale had prevented the Crown from passing the normal title to the premises under the law as it then was. The only person who could do that, apart from Edward Carleton, was Sir William Scawen who, as the Bankruptcy Commission's trustee, had authority to deal with the debtor's assets just as if they belonged to him. Being lord of the manor of Carshalton, Sir William was also entitled to fees for registering the copyhold part of the estate in the name of John Fellowes. So the latter, on the 31st October 1716 (probably after much haggling) finally paid over to Sir William £430 for the "Reversion and Inheritance and Equity of Redemption of the said freehold" and £430. 8s. 4d. for "the purchase of the said copyhold". (The deeds are in the Surrey Record Office and are very puzzling if one does not know what lay behind them.)

Another similarly puzzling thing is that none of the Carshalton House documents of title makes any mention at all of Dr. Radcliffe. As he never became legally the owner of the premises, the land deeds all make it appear that John Fellowes bought the property — for £7,663 — directly from the Crown; and what he actually paid the doctor's executors for it is not known. So, although historians of Carshalton have made much of the celebrated Dr. Radcliffe's connection with Carshalton House — and have even attributed the building of it to him — he never had anything to do with it, so far as the law is concerned.

CHAPTER FIVE
Sir John Fellowes

John Fellowes had the same sort of family background as Edward Carleton; they both belonged to the merchant class which was drawing constantly increasing wealth from England's ever-growing international trade. William Fellowes, John's father, was a London merchant who married the heiress of William Coulson, brother to Thomas Coulson, a director of the East India Company and also a Member of Parliament. John, being the fourth son, could not look forward to inheriting his father's wealth (though he did come into some of his uncle's estate), and the fortune he made must have been due largely to his own business acumen. Unlike Edward Carleton he did not specialise in one commodity, but was, in fact, more of a financier than a trader.

In the statement of his financial position which he had to render in 1721 he listed his commercial assets as follows:-

A share (varying from 1/16 to 1/30) in each of 12 ships £ 4,774. 10s. 0d.
18 Bottomries (i.e. mortgages on ships)   £16,450. 0s. 0d.
12 'Adventures' in cargoes and voyages   £ 6,114. 8s. 2d.
31 Loans   £11,853. 1s. 4d.

The only commodity in which he had made a substantial investment entirely on his own account was no ordinary merchandise, but "cocheneal", the red dye-stuff obtained from the crushed bodies of a South American species of beetle. Sir John had 4 bags containing 712 lbs. of this substance, but, if he was attempting to corner the market, he was unsuccessful, because, by March 1721 it was worth only £667. 10s., though he had paid £854. 3s. 3d. for it.

Of uncertain value were the insurance policies to which Fellowes had been a subscriber in those early 'Lloyd's Coffee House' days. As he pointed out in his statement "there may be losses" on those; but, equally, though he did not say so, there might be handsome profits. In any case, he would have been well able to meet any such liabilities out of the £11,310 he had in "Ready Money, Bank and Other Cash Notes", the £14,000 held in Exchequer Bills, and his £15,000 worth of "Malt and Land Tax Tallies" (i.e. money advanced to the government on the security of specified taxes). The only one of his 'gilts' whose value was doubtful was the £38,000 nominal of South Sea Company bonds (i.e., loan capital, not shares in the equity); but the rest of the portfolio, plus his cash in hand, was more than sufficient to cover the whole amount at risk on all his outstanding maritime

The lodge and entrance gates. The crowned lion's head, on the piers is the Fellowes' crest.

The Fellowes' arms in the 'Oak Room's' carved chimney-piece. The hand in the centre indicates a baronetcy.

'adventures' and loans — "on which great Losses may happen", he warned, once again without adding that they could also bring great gains.

That John Fellowes was, in fact, a very shrewd judge of a business risk is evidenced by the figure he put on "Debts due to me which are doubtful or desperate". They totalled a mere £620 and included £40 loaned to "Samuel Naylor, formerly my Servant, in low Circumstances" — a bad debt which introduces an apparently very human relationship in the midst of all the high finance.

Like most businessmen of his time, Fellowes had put money into real estate as well as commercial enterprises. Five freehold houses in Coleman Street, off London Wall, brought him in £98. 10s. per annum; in addition, he received £245. 6s. a year in rents from his Carshalton estate, which included Lower Mill (at £50), a Farm (at £48), a Malthouse and a dwelling house which went with it (at £24), and the 'Swan Inn' (at £18. 6s. 8d.).

To give modern equivalents for all Fellowes's assets is impossible because economic conditions have changed so much since his time, but there can be no doubt that his status among his contemporaries in the City of London was that of a present-day multi-millionaire. Nevertheless, because he did not personally operate the enterprises from which he drew his income, he was able to manage his financial empire from one room called "the Compting House" in his town residence; and his office staff consisted of one "book-keeper" whose salary was £100 a year. (But that was no pittance in the 18th century, as can be judged from the fact that Fellowes's own remuneration as Sub Governor of the South Sea Company was only £300 a year.)

His town house was in Old Jewry and had been taken, at a rental of £90 a year on a 36-year lease, in 1719, the year of his baronetcy and of his appointment as Sub Governor of the South Sea Company. When auctioned in 1723, the house was described as "large"; and it had "a Gateway leading from the Old Jewry, 75 Foot; a Courtyard 40 by 45 Foot; a Way leading to the Coach-House 36 Foot by 10 Foot; a small Back Yard with a Coach house adjoyning; and a Wash house." The house itself was three-storeyed, with a "Great Stair Case" and four rooms on each floor. Besides 'Parlours' and bedrooms, there were also a kitchen, a servants' hall, a butler's pantry, and "over the stables", a coachman's room and a footman's room. The total value of the contents shown in the inventory of 1721 was £604. 9s. (as against £753. 6s. 6d. for the contents of Carshalton House when owned by Fellowes).

If Sir John had kept to the sort of business he knew and understood, his financial position would have been impregnable; and it is quite clear that he could have had no idea what he was letting himself in for when he became involved with the South Sea Company. A history of Carshalton House is not the place for a detailed account of the affairs of that early state-sponsored commercial 'adventure'; but something must be said about Fellowes's part in it, in order to explain what happened to his country residence.

The South Sea Company was a consequence of the National Debt, which, at the time, was a comparatively new thing (previously the monarch had raised personal loans if he could not meet his administrative expenses out of revenue). Business morality being then rather primitive, governments did not, as now, regard borrowing as a way of life, but actually worried that they would have to settle their liabilities one day. Already, however, that was going to be an enormous undertaking; so to reduce its dimensions, the device was resorted to of making some of the loans permanent. This was done by having, first the Bank of England, and then the South Sea Company formed to take over part of the National Debt in return for a fixed interest payment plus certain commercial privileges. In the case of the South Sea Company these latter consisted of a trade monopoly with the Spanish colonies in the South Sea (i.e. the Pacific), guaranteed by a treaty between the Kings of England and Spain. The enterprise therefore needed backing at the highest level, and George I was, in fact, its titular Governor – though the effective executive head was the Sub Governor.

In 1718 the then Sub Governor of the South Sea Company died and John Fellowes, who was one of its directors, succeeded to the appointment – a tribute, no doubt, to his financial reputation at the time. A baronetcy soon followed; but so also did a big change in the scale of the Company's operations. It engaged itself to take over a great deal more of the National Debt and made large new issues of shares on the strength of its prospects. These caught the public imagination and the Company found itself able to charge a high premium for its new issue – and even higher premiums for further issues. All this amounted to a licence to print money, and full advantage was taken of it by the Directors and their friends (who included some very dubious characters attracted by the enormous profits to be made in share dealings).

The South Sea Company now became, in effect, a gigantic confidence trick which depended on the share price being pushed constantly upwards by expectations of huge profits. (Towards the end of its boom period the Directors, in a desperate attempt to avert the bursting of the 'Bubble', were actually promising dividends of 50% for 12 years.) There was, indeed, a solid base to the Company's operations, but it engaged in so many hazardous side-lines and made such extravagant commitments that there was bound to be a disastrous collapse when, as eventually happened, doubts about its future began to arise and share-holders started to sell. Within a very short time the price of its Stock had slumped from over £1,000 to £150, and ruin faced a lot of investors who had exchanged government securities for South Sea paper.

In the circumstances this could not be treated as just the failure of a private commercial enterprise, and the government of the day had to intervene. Official investigations into the affairs of the Company began, and, for a time, the Directors were held in custody in the Tower of London, for fear lest they abscond to the Continent. (The Company's Cashier, who was, effectively, its managing director, actually did just that, taking with him a 'green book' which contained the only record of a number of the Company's most questionable transactions.) Sir John's period of imprisonment in the Tower accounts for the following entry in the statement of affairs he later had to submit to a parliamentary committee: "February 24th 1721. Paid sundry Charges whilst in Custody of the Serjeant at Arms for Thirty one Days and upon my Discharge ... £121. 15s." – which indicates that the prisoner probably lived quite comfortably during his incarceration, but had to pay through the nose for the privilege.

The whole truth about the South Sea Company's business manoeuvres will never be known, because, although Knight, the Cashier, did eventually return to England and face questioning by a parliamentary 'Committee of Secrecy', the 'green book' was never seen again, and the most that could be got out of the witness was that "if he should disclose all he knew it would open such a scene as all the World would be amaz'd at." The Committee announced that "it has appeared to them throughout the Examinations yt [*that*] Mr. Knight, Cashier of the South Sea Company, is principally concerned in their most secret Transactions", but very little progress was made in finding out what exactly had been going on.

One thing became clear: there were false entries in the Company's books, and some of its money had disappeared without trace. Much of the missing cash had probably gone on what would nowadays be called 'slush' payments. In the 18th century, bribery to get parliamentary action in a required direction was not unusual, and it is likely that the South Sea Company had had to buy in some measure the statutory authority it needed for its operations. What is quite certain is that the favour of people with influence in state affairs had been obtained by the offer at par of shares which were fetching a vastly higher price in the market. During the investigations which followed the ultimate bursting of the 'Bubble', Sir John Fellowes was closely questioned about some of these transactions and said that "whilst the proposal of the South Sea Company and the Bill was depending in the house of Commons, Mr. Knight told him that Mr. Sec.Y Craggs [*one of the two principal Ministers of the Crown at the time*] propos'd that £12,000 of the Company's stock should be disposed of to the Duchess of Kendal, £12,000 to the Countess of Platen, and £12,000 to the Duchesses 2 Neices [*sic*]". Sir John admitted that he agreed to this proposal, but, according to him, on condition that they paid "the market price which was then above £150". He went on to say that, later on, he visited the Duchess to request "her good offices in the Company's behalf", and "She wrote a letter signifying her acceptance, but he had lost the letter." (The Duchess of Kendal and the Countess of Platen were the official titles of George I's two German mistresses, but, by their physical characteristics — which spoke volumes for the catholicity of the King's tastes — they were known to the British public as respectively the Dumpling and the Maypole.)

In matters concerning the South Sea Company's affairs Sir John Fellowes was capable of losing his memory as well as a Duchess's letter. When questioned about another allocation of shares made in very dubious circumstances, "he said that he did not know of any particular parcel of Stock holden by Turner and Company untill lately, and said that he did not remember the Disposal of ye £50,000 Stock to them". But, in fairness, it must be said that at one stage during his interrogation he pleaded that "I was in the Spring and in the Summer, very much affected in my head and am so still . . . . I have been much affected as to my memory".

It is impossible now to gauge the extent of the Sub Governor's responsibility for what went wrong with the South Sea Company. In the Commons it was said that he was "not so active in the late vile and pernicious practices as some others, owing perhaps rather to the heaviness than the purity of his mind". But the statements of their financial affairs filed with Parliament by all the Company's Directors showed Sir John Fellowes to have been by far the wealthiest of them all; so, on the principle that a fool and his money are soon parted, he cannot have been all that dim-witted. More probably he was out of his depth in the comparatively new world of share certificates and paper values — as were many of his fellow merchants who had made their money out of shoes and ships and sealing wax and such-like solid saleables. Even Sir William Scawen, Fellowes's Carshalton neighbour and an ex-Governor of the Bank of England, took shares in the South Sea Company, which, as his will put it, had "fallen short of Expectations".

Sir John Fellowes himself, in his statement of affairs, emphasised that shortly before the Company collapsed he had increased his holdings of its Stock, being left in March 1721 with a nominal £86,436 worth, as against £69,757 worth on the 1st June 1720. This would, indeed, seem to indicate that, right until the end, the Sub Governor still had faith in the Company's future. But that would be to over-simplify the situation. Collating all the relevant entries in the chronological account of Sir John's income and expenditure, it appears that in all he paid cash or securities to the value of some £170,000 for Stock. (But £41,700 of this was "in the Names of several Persons from whom I can expect no repayment", and what other consideration he might have received to prompt this apparent generosity one is left to guess). Against the £170,000 there must be set receipts totalling £164,000 from the sale of Stock to a nominal value of £22,000 at prices varying from £535 to £840 per £100 unit. The holding the Sub Governor was left with was, then, really in the nature of a bonus, he, as a prudent business-man, having played the market very successfully to cover himself against any substantial loss.

Parliament met the South Sea disaster by passing a 'Sufferers' Act' designed to obtain reimbursement of the losses of innocent persons from all those deemed to have been at fault in the handling of the Company's affairs. In Sir John Fellowes's case the intention of the Act was to leave him with £10,000, but all the rest of his property was to be confiscated and sold. 'South Sea' documents in the House of Lords Record Office (already quoted from) include a report from the 'Trustees for the sale of Directors' Estates', which shows that, by February 1723 there had been realised from the Sub Governor's personalty the sum of £127,730. 4s. 3d., while sales of his real estate had yielded a further £25,560. This was, by a long way, the largest individual contribution to the total of roughly £1,400,000 collected at that date. (Ultimately over £2,000,000 was recovered.)

Sir John Fellowes probably continued to live in Carshalton House (he certainly died in it), although the whole of the former Carleton estate came, technically into the possession of the 'Sufferers' Trustees and was sold by them. The price paid was £14,310, nearly twice what the property had fetched in 1714. The land and buildings which went with Carshalton House could hardly have been improved to this extent. The increase must have been largely due to additions made to the mansion and its grounds, on which, in the inventory of 1721, Sir John had put a value of £3,500 "as it cost me" (i.e. without adding anything for improvements).

The purchaser of Sir John's Carshalton estate was his younger brother, Edward, who, in the land deeds, is described as either a Gentleman or a Mercer. But the Mercers' Company have no record of him; and, in the *Gentleman's Magazine's* report of his death in 1731 he is said to have been "formerly Master in Chancery". (The eldest Fellowes brother, William, had been a Senior Master in the Chancery Court.) In Sir John's statement of affairs Edward is shown to have been lent — and subsequently repaid — the sum of £300. This does not suggest that the younger brother would have been in a position three years later to buy an estate worth £14,000; and one cannot help suspecting that the money came actually from the resources of the late Sub Governor of the South Sea Company — even although he was supposed to have had only £10,000 left to live on. He would not be unique as a failed financier who had managed to salt enough away to maintain his standard of living.

But there was one thing Sir John could not buy: health. On the 26th July 1724, two days after the Carshalton estate had been formally conveyed to his younger brother, he died at the comparatively early age of fifty-four. There is no record of what his death was attributed to by contemporary medical opinion; but it may be significant that two items in his account of expenditure were: £7. 7s. for "Spaw *[Spa]* Water" and £55. 6s. for the settlement of an apothecary's bill. Was Sir John Fellowes affected in the same way as many modern business-men are by the pressures of his way of life? Did he suffer from stomach ulcers, or hypertension, or coronary degeneration? Certainly he was spending on his health what were, for those days, very substantial sums of money. But there is no hint, in any surviving document, that he was leading a dissipated life. In fact, he seems to have devoted himself just to making money — though he did spend 2 guineas on a book during the nine months period of his statement of affairs. He died unmarried and made no financial provisions which would suggest that he had kept a mistress. He does not seem to have indulged in extravagant expenditure on personal adornment either; the only item of that nature he recorded was a payment of £29. 1s. off a haberdasher's bill for £33. 3s. And the only articles of jewellery in his list of possessions were "one ring set with 11 small diamonds, bought 1707", "a Gold Snuff Box which I have had several years", "a Gold Watch which I have also had several Years" and "one ring set with a large Diamond which was the Ring of my honour'd Uncle, Thomas Coulson, who died 1713."

Of course, Sir John Fellowes lived very comfortably; but there is no sign of ostentatious expenditure in his statement of affairs — apart from what he spent on improving Carshalton House. (In the 9 months covered by his accounts, he paid his steward, in all, £1,008. 19s. "most of which was for Work and Materials for my House and Garden at Carshalton".) "About £1500" he put as "Paid Household Expences in Town, Parish Duties etc., Cloaths for myself and Servants, and my Pocket Expenses" during that same period. The wages bill for his staff was certainly very modest: on the 21st March, for remuneration due up to "Christmas last", his butler received £27. 11s. 8d., Sarah Brett (presumably his housekeeper) £22. 13s. 8d., his footman £15. 6s. 8d., his groom £12. 7s. 8d., his coachman £10. 14s. 6d., his cook £8 and his housemaid £6. Charles Caesar, his black servant, must have been acquired (? how) shortly after these payments were made; the Carshalton parish registers record his baptism on the 1st May 1721 and his burial in November 1728 (? a victim of our climate).

Sir John Fellowes's will, dated the 2nd November 1723, was proved with a sworn statement from Samuel Reeves, his steward, that he had witnessed the death, and that afterwards Edward Fellowes "opened an Escriptore in the said Deced's Chamber and in one of the Drawers found the Will which was obliterated in the Second and third Lines as now appeareth". It is impossible to make out what was written under the obliteration, but the next words are "to my sister ffellowes many thanks for the continuance of her Civilities since my Misfortunes and desire her acceptance of fifty guineas for a legacy." There may be some sarcasm here (and some others which Sir John decided to erase), because he bequeathed his married sister £50 a year, his three nephews got £100 apiece, and two nieces received £500 each, with a direction that their father was "not to intermedle therewith". (Sir John seems almost to have been an early feminist, for another legacy of £25 a year to a married woman was accompanied by a proviso that her husband was "not to concern himself therewith", and, if he did, the legacy was to be void.)

A number of cousins, friends and their children received lump sums ranging from £300 to £10. The "Rev. Mr. Hollier", rector of Carshalton got £20, but £100 went to Phineas Pett "whom I putt to Sea". That latter bequest sounds to have been a charitable one; and there were a number which were definitely of that character. One hundred pounds was to be paid to each of "the three great hospitals in London: Christ's, St. Bartholomew's and Bridewell"; £100 to "the Charity Commissioners of the Old Jewry parish"; another £100 to "the Charity Children of Colledge Hill"; £20 each to the poor of the three parishes of "Colledge Hill, St. Antholins and the Old Jewry"; and £30 to the poor of Carshalton.

Sir John thought of his servants, too — even the lowliest of them. At the top of the list, naturally, came Samuel Reeves, who got £80 "betwixt him and his wife". The gardener, Cuthbert Hopper and his wife shared £70, while their daughter Sarah was to get another £30 "or if she is deceased to go amongst their other children". Twenty pounds went to each of the "Men Servants and Maid Servants living with me at my decease"; but the housekeeper, Mary Allen received an annuity of £20. All the servants were "to have Mourning and all to be continued in their places for one year from my decease". There were also bequests of £10 each to four men "that have usually work'd in my Grounds", and £5 to each House "amongst all the Workmen of our several Sugar Houses". But the most 'human' of the provisions made for Sir John's servants was £100 to "Charles Caesar, my Indian Boy, who may be destitute when I am gone, to place him out in the world, and I also give him £5 per annum annuity whilst he continue with my Relations". (As already mentioned, Charles Caesar survived his master by only four years.)

The total of the bequests made by this will was over £5,000, with, in addition, £175 a year in annuities. It reads as the testament of a generous man who was loyal to his family, fond of children and had consideration for those who worked for him. But it does not sound as though Sir John had only £10,000 to his name. "All the rest and residue of my Estate" he bequeathed to "my loveing Brother Edward ffellowes of St. Paul's, Covent Garden", whom he also appointed sole executor "not doubting his punctuality and honour in the performance thereof". And, finally, Sir John showed his affection for Carshalton by directing that, wherever he died, he should be buried there "privately but decently". Before he bought Carshalton House he had had other plans for a final resting place; in the City church of St. Michael's Paternoster Royal, an inscription announced: "Underneath is the vault belonging to the family of William Fellowes of Lincoln's Inn, Esq., *[Sir John's eldest brother]* and of Mr. John Fellowes of London, merchant, brothers. Ann. Dom. 1712".

Edward Fellowes came to live in Carshalton House and proceeded to do his testamentary benefactor's memory proud. Sir William Scawen and Sir John Fellowes together had earlier paid for a gallery to be erected in Carshalton church for the accommodation of their households during services. Edward now, in return for permission to place a memorial to his brother in the north aisle, had to agree to "make the North side of the said Church answerable to and in like manner as the south side", to quote from the Vestry's minute book; and he was also required to charge Lower Mill (then "the Copper Mill") with an annual payment of £20 for the benefit of the poor of the parish. With the Vestry's blessing Edward Fellowes then set about filling the east end of the north aisle with a vast monument in veined marble on which was inscribed only the name, title, date of death and age of his brother. No doubt, because of the South Sea Company's failure, it was considered best to say nothing at all about Sir John's achievements. Following a rebuilding of the church in the late nineteenth century Sir John Fellowes's memorial, together with a quite modest one recording Edward's own death in 1730 (1731 N.S.), was moved to the west end of the outer south aisle, where it now faces the even more impressive monument to Sir William Scawen and his wife, still in its original position at the east end.

But a huge slab of marble in the church and a Charity which helped many a Carshalton youngster to be apprenticed to a trade, were not the only mementoes left of Sir John's life in the parish. As will appear in the next chapter, the additions he made to his residence can still be seen and now make Carshalton House unique among the surviving buildings of its period. It had not, however, been Sir John's original intention to end his days in the house he had acquired in 1715. His 1721 statement of affairs noted a debt of "about £68,000 due on Contract for Mrs. Titus's Estate if same proceed". Mrs. Titus, after the death in 1704 of her husband Col. Silius Titus, had inherited his manor of Ramsey in Huntingdonshire, but, evidently, the South Sea Company's débâcle made it impossible for Sir John Fellowes to complete the purchase of that property (which was worth nearly ten times what the Carleton estate had cost Dr. Radcliffe). Mrs. Titus did not, in fact, sell her estate to anyone, and it passed eventually to a daughter who died unmarried in 1732 leaving everything she had to be divided between a male servant and a female servant. The manorial land was then valued at £2,000 a year; and, by what seems to have been a pure coincidence, it was bought in 1737 by Coulson Fellowes who had, in the meantime, inherited Carshalton House from his uncle Edward. (Ramsey remained in the possession of the Fellowes family and the present Lord de Ramsey is a descendant of Coulson Fellowes.)

Sir John Fellowes had had to be content with having, in less than ten years, nearly doubled the value of Carshalton House and the land which went with it.

CHAPTER SIX

The making of a 'handsom Seat'

The inventories which were taken respectively of Edward Carleton's and Sir John Fellowes's possessions in Carshalton House show that the life style of the two men was almost exactly the same. It seems that either Carleton lived beyond his means or Fellowes saved a lot of his income, because the latter was by far the richer man, and could not have been ruined, as Carleton was, by debts totalling £30,000. Only in two respects do the inventories suggest that Fellowes was significantly a 'warmer' man. For transport he had a coach, two chariots, "an old Chaise", 6 coach horses, 4 saddle horses and 3 cart horses – as against Carleton's complement of 7 horses, a coach and a chariot. And, whereas no silver articles at all appear in the Carleton lists, Fellowes had, in Carshalton House, candlesticks, salt cellars, spoons and other plate weighing in all 160 ounces, with a further 315 ounces in his town house.

In the equipment of their living rooms, however, the two men had not merely similar standards, they had, to a large extent, (as Sister Pauline Stevens noticed) precisely the same furniture. Of course, the Carleton assets which Dr. Radcliffe had bid for had included the contents of the mansion, and his executors would have had no reason to separate the furniture from the rest of the property when selling to Fellowes. Even so, it is remarkable that, though the wealthier man did add some valuable items to the furnishings of the house, the total value of the contents was roughly the same in 1721 as it had been in 1713.

For my own satisfaction I have set out, side by side, the furnishing correspondences in the two inventories, but I do not propose to inflict this rather dull tabulation on the reader. What is interesting, though, is that it enables room identifications to be made, for the correspondences reveal that the inventory takers followed similar routes in their tour of the premises. On the ground floor they both began with the great staircase and hall. But the "2 Closetts" which figure next in the Carleton inventory and at that time housed a miscellany of articles, appear (in the same position) in the Fellowes inventory as "Butler's Pantry" (in which there were a "copper Monteth" *[a large bowl]* and a square table) and "Mr. Reeve's Closet" (which evidently served as the steward's office since it contained "a Wallnut-wood Scrutore *[a writing desk]* , two old Chairs and Lumber").

After the closets, the two inventories list, in the same order, four rooms which can be identified as the Painted Parlour, the Oak Room, the remaining

Parlour on the east side of the house, and the Common Parlour (later the 'Adam' room); after which come the kitchen and back kitchen. This would be the natural sequence in which to visit the ground floor rooms for anyone who started from a central hall and staircase (which had 'Closets' adjacent to the stairs) and worked his way round to the passage leading to the domestic offices on the west of the building. He would have found three Parlours opening off the hall on one side of it, while, on the other side, would have been the Common Parlour and, beyond it, a 'passage' which has since been made into an entrance hall. That lay-out of the ground floor would explain why there is no mention in either inventory of the two rooms which now occupy the centre of the building, and why one has to go through one or other of those two rooms to get into the 'Parlours' on the east side of the house. Further support for this 'reconstruction' of the original ground floor plan comes from the fact that the now divided room to the north of the present entrance hall is known to have once been a kitchen. (Sister Pauline Stevens discovered in the wall traces of what appeared to be an old flue leading to an oven.)

There are statements in print that the main entrance to the mansion was originally through the door in the middle of the south front, but, unfortunately, they are not contemporary with that state of the premises. When Carshalton House was advertised for sale in 1839 the catalogue described the central "Drawing room, saloon or library", into which the door then led, as "formerly the saloon and state entrance of the mansion." And, in the *Victoria County History*, it is stated that "the principal entrance opened into a large panelled hall now used as the library." This would, of course, have been in accordance with standard architectural practice in the early 18th century. Furthermore, a 'Queen Anne' house is unlikely to have been built with a central hall from which there was no direct access to the first floor. The 'great staircase' was, in those days, a prominent feature in a gentleman's residence; and, although the present main staircase of Carshalton House is an elegant 18th century construction, it is, as Charles Barrett wrote, "not in a position where its beauty can be properly appreciated"; moreover, it is far from the old 'state entrance'.

On the first floor, the room identifications by furniture are made easy by the reappearance in the Fellowes inventory of the wrought, chintz, red damask and blue damask beds which figured in the Carleton inventory. Both lists finished with what, in 1713, was called "Madam Carleton's room". But in that year the inventory takers went clockwise, beginning with the "furthest Roome on the Stairs", while, in 1721, they went anti-clockwise, beginning with the Chintz Room. There is only one possible location for the Carleton "Roome at the End of the Gallery", and, taking that as a fixed point, Madam Carleton turns out to have slept in the central north-facing bedroom. Any inventory takers coming up a central stairway would have found it natural to begin their task at this spot and then work round the gallery, visiting each bedroom in turn. And the fact that, in 1713, they started with the room to the left of Madam Carleton's, whereas, in 1721, they chose the one to the right of it may have been due to either chance or personal left-handedness or right-handedness respectively – or to the fact that they had come up on different sides of a branching staircase.

There is, incidentally, a very remarkable correspondence in the furnishings of one of the rooms on the first floor: Edward Carleton had a room without a bed in it, which was adorned with 70 prints and 36 pieces of china ware; John

42

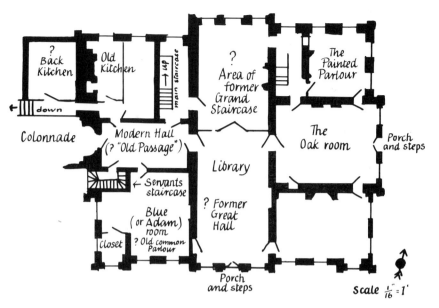

The ground floor of the mansion.

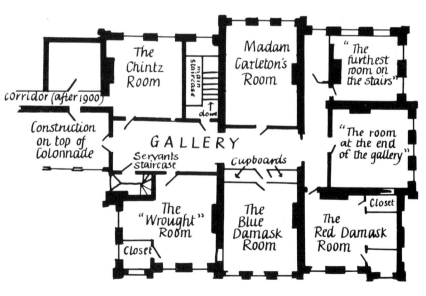

The first floor of the mansion with suggested 'Carleton' room identifications.

43

Fellowes, too, had a bedless room, and in it were displayed 56 black and white prints and 16 pieces of china. It looks as if a 'bedroom' with this kind of decoration served some purpose which was fashionable at the time.

On the top floor the modest nature of most of the furnishings makes it difficult to identify rooms by correspondences in the two inventories. But "Madam Skinner's Room" appears to have become a "Maid's Garrett" in Sir John's time, while the bedroom of "Madam Mary" (Carleton) matches "Mr. Reeve's Room" in the 1721 inventory. That latter transformation still preserved a high social status for the room, because Samuel Reeves, the steward, was a most important member of the Fellowes household, responsible for the day to day running of the whole Carshalton estate. He seems also to have constituted himself the armed guardian of the premises, for his room had acquired since Madam Mary's time "a Blunderbuss and a Musketoon" — though it is doubtful how much use those antique weapons would have been, except as frighteners.

In the remaining part of the mansion, the basement, it is not possible, from either inventory, to visualise exactly the divisions of the area, but Sir John Fellowes seems to have brought more of it into use. For one thing, he had an extra storage place for the household's drink, since there were now listed a "Strong Beer Cellar" (containing six casks, thirteen barrels and five stillings [cask stands]); a "Small Beer Cellar" (with the same number of receptacles); and a "Bottle Cellar" (which held three bins, fifty dozen glass bottles, racks and a lead cistern). Sir John appears also to have given his domestic staff improved conditions, because there is mention in the 1721 inventory of a "Servants' Hall" in the basement — though it was furnished only with "a Grate, Fender and Fire-Shovel, two Tables, three Forms and a Napkin Press". In the basement, too, at this time there was a "Laundry" fitted with "a Grate and a Stove for Heaters". The Washhouse was still in the same position, next to the Brewhouse, so the Laundry was probably used for ironing. There was much more of that to do now, for the Fellowes' inventory lists "fifteen pair of Servants' Sheets, ten pair of fine Sheets and one pair of Callico Sheets — as against a 1713 grand total of six pairs which were not "foul"; and Sir John also had more towels and table linen than Edward Carleton. Under "Linnen", too, in 1721, comes — very oddly — "a large Carpet in the best Parlour" (where Carleton had only a "matt").

The Dairy, which came immediately after the back kitchen in the Carleton inventory, seems to have become a Larder in 1721 (no cows are listed in the Fellowes inventory), because there is now mention of bedding in "Rooms over the Larder". Sir John, on the other hand, had no furniture in the room over the Brewhouse, though, somewhere else, there were a Coachman's room and a Groom's room, both very sparsely furnished as bedrooms. The many exact correspondences in the two inventories, however, make it quite plain that Edward Carleton's house was not pulled down and rebuilt. That would, indeed, have been a pointless thing to do — unless, of course, the accommodation was increased; but it is precisely the same in both inventories.

Apart from minor changes in furnishings, there is actually only one room in the mansion which unmistakeably and importantly owes something to Sir John Fellowes. That room was the principal drawing-room, which is now called the Oak Room because it is entirely panelled with that wood. What identifies it with the Fellowes occupation of the premises is a finely carved oak chimney-piece, incorporating Sir John's arms. (The significance of this piece of ornamentation seems to have been forgotten at one time, because the compiler of the 1839 sale catalogue wrote: "This room *[then the Dining Room]* is a striking feature of the house . . . with a curious *[!]* Marble and carved Chimney Piece.")

Another of the artistic treasures of Carshalton House, the Painted Parlour, has also for long been assumed to have been a Fellowes creation. But since Sister Pauline Stevens's researches have established, as already mentioned, that the marine picture in this room was apparently executed before 1707, responsibility for the whole decorative scheme is more likely to rest on Edward Carleton. The room was certainly described as "the Painted Parlour" in the inventory of his possessions. It is possible, of course, that not all the paintings were done at the same time; and, indeed, Sister Pauline Stevens spotted that two on one of the doors were dated 1873 and initialled "C.R.R.B." — clearly the work of Charles Barrett and a sort of profanation of the original decoration which one would not have expected of him.

Although once fashionable, not many rooms of this kind have survived in England, but 'Littlecote', a mansion near Hungerford, has a so-called 'Dutch Parlour', the panelled walls of which are covered with paintings done by Dutch prisoners taken in the naval battles of the 1660s. The subjects of the pictures and the style of execution in the 'Littlecote' room are nothing like those in the one in Carshalton House; but it seems that this was a Dutch fashion in interior decoration, which was probably brought 'officially' to England following William III's accession to the throne, and remained modish during the early years of Queen Anne's reign. Mr. Derek Sherborn, who contributed an article on Carshalton House to the issue of *Country Life* dated the 4th March 1949, wrote in it: "The artist responsible for the Carshalton paintings . . . is unknown, but they have a Dutch flavour about them". However, some time before George I became King of England in 1714, the country had ceased to look to Holland for a lead in fashion, and it was by virtue of a Patent from the first of the Hanoverians that the Sub Governor of the South Sea Company had acquired Carshalton House. All the circumstances, then, suggest that the Painted Parlour is more likely to date from the Carleton, rather than the Fellowes, occupation of the building.

So what, after all this, did Sir John Fellowes do to account for the statement in the 'Aubrey' book on Surrey that "he is now *[c. 1718]* about building a handsom Seat."? The truth is that, apart from the Oak Room, all his creations lie outside the main block of the mansion. However, the first of them — geographically — immediately adjoins it on the west side. What the Carleton inventory calls the "passage" leading to the domestic offices becomes in the Fellowes inventory, "The passage to the Colonnade" (and in it there were a fowling piece, two carbines and 36 water buckets — precautions, presumably against both fire and robbery). This Colonnade — still visible, though in a much altered state — appears to have been constructed as an ornamental feature (probably roofed) to link the house with the brewery, wash-house and stables. But the open spaces between the stone columns of the Colonnade were later filled in and another storey imposed on it, so that it now looks to be an architecturally eccentric extension of the mansion's living accommodation.

As late as 1839, however, when Carshalton House was up for sale, the carriage drive was described by the auctioneers as terminating "at a broad circular

Flight of Stone Steps and handsome colonnade, forming a fine vestibule and entrée to the mansion", while, to the west, there was "a Range of offices extending from the Colonnade and presenting a handsome Wing with Arched Gateway in the Centre to the Courtyard within". It had been an ingenious adaptation of Fellowes's Colonnade to make it the principal entrance to the mansion, but that was not its original function, for, as already mentioned, the 1839 sale particulars themselves locate the former "state entrance" in the middle of the south front. Incidentally, the "Range of offices" in 1839 comprised a "Store room and Bed Room over; a Complete brewhouse, Wash house and laundry; a Dairy and Scullery for ditto"; together with, in the yard, "an Ornamental Dove House" — all exactly what stood on the site in the early 18th century (but now replaced by school and convent buildings which belong to the 'St. Philomena's' era).

When, in 1740, the premises had been insured (further details of this are given in the next chapter), the house itself, valued at £1750, together with "the Wash House, Brew House and Colonnade", valued at £250, were included in one policy, while a second one was required to cover separately "a Building ½ Brick and ½ Timber, being Coach House, Stables & Barns, and Wood House", valued at £700. From this it would appear that the transport unit was then no longer connected with the domestic offices but was already housed in the detached block of buildings which, round a courtyard, lay between the west side of the carriage drive and Shorts Road and was still standing at the beginning of this century. In the 1839 sale catalogue it figured as "A Handsome uniform range of Substantial Stabling in character with the Mansion, with a Gate in the Centre, surmounted by a Cupola, Turret Clock and Vane." This "uniform range" offered, at that time, the following accommodation: "2 stables containing 6 stalls; 2 or 3 large loose Hunter's Boxes; Harness and Saddle Rooms; Standing for several Carriages, with large double circular Doors; Sleeping room for Grooms and Hay lofts". And the "spacious Stable and cattleyard" was also fronted by "a Cart house, a large Barn, Cow houses fitted up with Racks etc.; open Sheds and Poultry houses."

According to Charles Barrett, the late 19th century owner-historian of Carshalton House, the creator of this stable block was Sir John Fellowes, but the evidence on which that assertion was based was not stated. The inventory of 1721 does not record Fellowes as a keeper of cattle (and no cowhouse is mentioned in the 1740 insurance policy), but he certainly had more horses and carriages to house than had Carleton; and no other owner of Carshalton House between 1724 and 1740 appears likely to have built such an expensive addition to the premises as the stable block in question. In all probability then, Sir John Fellowes is rightly credited with having introduced it into his "handsom Seat". He was, however, no farmer; for, whereas the Carleton inventory listed livestock and crops, the 1721 one showed only: "In the Barn: some Corn and some Hay; two Carts, Fire-Wood and Lumber."

It must be said, though, that there may have been omissions from the Fellowes inventory. Certainly it is difficult to explain the complete absence of horticultural implements from it, for there is good evidence that his garden meant a lot to Sir John and he spent a great deal of money on creating one in what was then a very new style. His account of expenditure between June 1720 and March 1721 shows that Joseph Carpenter & Co. were paid £200 for trees, Nicholas Parker, also for trees, was paid £23. 2s., and Charles Bridgman received £138 for unstated goods or services. (The last-named also received later, by Sir John's will, a legacy of 10 guineas.) Probably, at the time, nobody would have needed telling what Bridgman had to offer. He was a designer of gardens who is known to have worked at Hampton Court, Windsor, Newmarket and Richmond; he also invented the boundary device called the ha-ha, and held the official appointment of Keeper of Bushey Park. Bridgman was, in fact, a pioneer in the English style of landscape gardening which was later to be brought to perfection by 'Capability' Brown; and it seems that Sir John Fellowes, with artistically placed trees and shrubs, was aiming to give Carshalton House a setting in the height of fashion – and one whose basic features are still in evidence to-day. A further instance of care for his garden may be indicated, too, by the £149. 16s. he paid for "Statuary" to Robert Hartshorne, whose monument to Bishop Burnet in St. James's Church, Clerkenwell, shows that, in his time, he was highly regarded as a sculptor. It cannot be definitely stated that what he contributed to Carshalton House was garden statuary, but a mid-eighteenth century letter, quoted in the next chapter, refers to a statue in the grounds; and there still remains near the house a sundial in the form of a large stone classical urn which could date back to the days of Sir John Fellowes.

Because he was for so long looked on as the "onlie begetter" of Carshalton House, practically everything antique about it does tend to get attributed to Sir John; so, naturally, its 'grotto' has always been taken to have been his creation. There is actually no documentary evidence to connect him with it; but, having regard to his proved desire to beautify his garden and the exactly contemporary fashion for 'grottos', this construction can, with fair certainty, be regarded as another element in the "handsom Seat" he created. In 1724 Thomas Scawen, who had inherited Carshalton Park from his uncle, Sir William Scawen, had a grotto built to his own design at the head of the watercourse in the Park, and this was probably an attempt to 'keep up with the Felloweses'. The Carshalton House grotto (oddly called by the *Victoria County History* "a stone garden house") is situated beside the lake, near the spring-head – a location somewhat similar to that of the Carshalton Park one. But unlike the latter, which is brick built, the Carshalton House construction was in some kind of stone (which, from the whiteness it has preserved, makes me wonder whether it is actually clunch – the hard chalk once commonly used locally in building). There is, however, a similarity between the two grottos in one respect: each had earth heaped on top of it to give the required effect of excavated antiquity. (Robert Adam later wrote: "the Italians give to ruins dug up and cleared the name of grotto".)

The Carshalton House grotto contains a number of passages, together with a round chamber, and it was called the 'Hermitage' – presumably to indicate that it was intended to represent a dwelling-place of holy anchorites. Some 18th century gentlemen actually added romantic interest to their grounds by employing someone to live as a 'hermit' in a grotto, but it is not known whether this ever happened at Carshalton House. There is, in fact, no reason to suppose that the 'Hermitage' there was put to any use at all until the Daughters of the Cross acquired the estate. They put up, in its interior, plaques commemorating a number of Superiors of the Convent, converted the principal chamber into an oratory, and erected on top of the building a statue of the Virgin. But the years have taken their toll of the Hermitage, and 'Danger' notices now forbid close inspection. The building's complete collapse would mean the loss of a picturesque survival of 18th century romanticism, which, unlike its counterpart in Carshalton Park, still exhibits its original appearance and building materials. Not many of these once fashionable 'follies' have been preserved, and, as they were always highly individual, Carshalton House possesses in its Hermitage something, quite literally, unique.

It is unlikely that all the Fellowes' beautifications of the grounds of Carshalton House would have been undertaken if these had still been traversed by a public footpath. And not only is there no mention of any such right of way after the end of the 17th century, but a high wall was built to guarantee privacy to the owner of the mansion. It seems certain that Sir John was responsible for the building of this wall because it is obviously contemporary with the gateway to his carriage drive, and that is unquestionably identified with him by the stone crowned lions (the Fellowes crest) on the pillars which flank the wrought iron gates. (The Fellowes' motifs which those latter also originally exhibited were omitted when, owing to the ravages of time, a modern reproduction had to be substituted for the 18th century ironwork.)

The present lodge beside the main entrance, which, in the Convent's early days, housed its Chaplain for a time, is either an enlargement or a replacement of an earlier, much smaller, building. (In the 1839 sale catalogue it is described as "Brick and Slated" with "3 rooms, Pantry etc.".) But the wall which runs from the gates − in one direction along Carshalton Road and Shorts Road, and in the other along Pound Street and part of West Street − still displays its original brickwork, though repairs have been necessary in places. Once again, because of Sir John's acquisition of the Carleton brickyard, Carshalton bricks may have been used in the building of this wall.

It is when the wall reaches West Street that there is made manifest the disappearance of that public right of way through the grounds of Carshalton House which is marked on the 'Arundel' map. Old water-colours by Yates, dating from the early 1800s, show that, from the former 'Swan Inn' to Pound Street, there then ran alongside the wall a raised causeway for pedestrians − though all the rest of the present first part of West Street remained a large sheet of water which horses and vehicles had to ford. Did the foot causeway come into existence at the same time as the wall, or did it represent an earlier solution to the old public right of way problem, with the wall merely following an already accepted boundary? That is a conundrum which cannot be answered on the available evidence.

The whole question does, however, seem to be connected with what happened to the lake in the grounds. In the 18th century it was clearly not all one with the water which stretched across the south end of West Street − as it appears to have been at the time of the 'Arundel' map. And, from the spring head, it no longer followed its 'Arundel' easterly course, but ran roughly northwards, terminating in a flint and rubble construction intended to look like a bridge and in style somewhat resembling the grotto at the other end of the lake. Enhancing the picturesqueness of that water there also came into existence an island which does not appear on the 'Arundel' map. However, what is most 'contrived' about the Carshalton House water in the 18th century is the use made of it. And the man responsible for introducing that use was undoubtedly Sir John Fellowes. There had obviously been a lake in Carleton's time, because the inventory shows him to have possessed two boats. But he had nothing corresponding to what Sir John called a "Greenhouse and Bagnio" − a building which was actually much more than that,

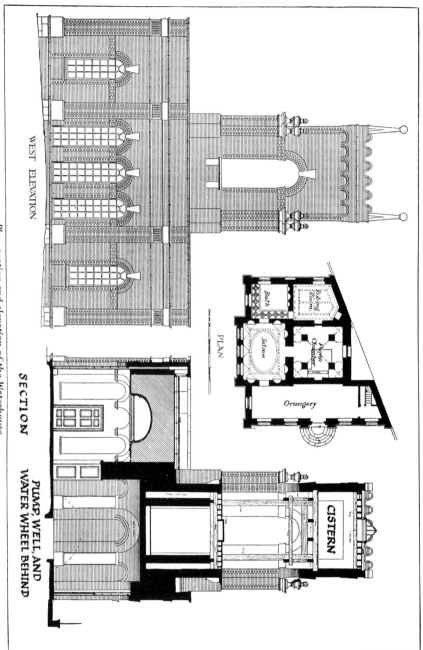

WEST ELEVATION

PLAN

SECTION

Bath

Dressing Room

Saloon

Pump Chamber

Orangery

PUMP, WELL, AND
WATER WHEEL BEHIND

CISTERN

Plan, section and elevation of the Waterhouse.

49

and through which the outfall of the lake was artificially channelled.

This structure — since called the Waterhouse — is, architecturally and archaeologically, the most valuable part of the Carshalton House heritage, because, although not unusual in its time, it is probably a unique survival in present-day England. Little changed in appearance since it was first built, the Waterhouse fronts — or, more accurately, backs — directly onto West Street, with its rear elevation continuing the line (and the brick courses) of Fellowes's estate wall. A clue to its prime function is provided by the tall, strongly built, central tower; but, although that function was still being performed until quite recently, the *Victoria County History*, published early in this century, considered that "its original purpose is not quite apparent". A century previously it had been well-known. In *"A Companion from London to Brightelmston"* James Edwards had written: "Near the middle of the lawn is a canal with a handsome waterhouse or conduit at its east end, from whence the house is supplied with water." And the sale particulars of 1839 enlarged on this with the information that the tower contained "The well-constructed Water Works and large Reservoir lined with Lead (containing several thousand Gallons), from which the top of the Mansion and all the offices, Stables etc. are copiously supplied with Water."

The "Water Works" consisted of pumping machinery powered by a water wheel which was turned by the outfall of the lake as it flowed through the building. (The stream then passed under the pedestrian causeway outside and helped to form the pond which covered the entrance to West Street.) When, in 1949, Mr. Derek Sherborn described Carshalton House for *Country Life* the lake was already dry and he thought that the water which ran under the Waterhouse fell into the lake. But he is not likely to have been mistaken when he wrote: "The engine now remaining is incomplete but is said to date from 1784". That date seems to come from the book by Field and Bunney, already mentioned; it is, of course, long after Sir John Fellowes's time, but, even in the 18th century, machinery did not last for ever. Alas, due to the installation of a central heating plant for school purposes, the only vestiges now to be seen — and that not easily — of the old pumping apparatus, are the water channel and some skeletal spokes of the wheel. Electricity had, some time earlier, been substituted for water as the power which drove it upwards. But, in Charles Barrett's time, there were "three old fashioned but powerful plunge pumps driven by a 14 foot water wheel."

Water from a lake had not been good enough for a wealthy 18th century household to drink; what was pumped up into the "large Reservoir" on the roof of the tower came through pipes direct from the spring head. (The elaborate brick culverts at that site probably date from Fellowes's time; they strongly resemble those under the grotto in Carshalton Park.) From the top of the tower the drinking water was conveyed by the force of gravity through further piping to the mansion and all its ancillary buildings. This, in the 1720s, would have been the height of luxury, to be enjoyed only by the very rich. Even in 1839 it was something to be expatiated on; the sale catalogue of that date, amplifying the description of the "Water Works" already quoted, said: "Every Part of the Mansion, Offices, Yards etc, are *[sic]* supplied with Soft and Spring Water by means of capacious Tanks and Cisterns and various Pumps."

This seems an appropriate place at which to refer to a suggestion made — and apparently believed by Dr. Peatling — that there was once a mill driven by the waters of the Carshalton House lake. His notes report that during a dry summer in the early 1920s "the bed of the present lake was exposed, and foundations of an old mill and sluice were laid bare, with remains of massive oak beams and some very large nails." Photographs which Dr. Peatling took at the time show brickwork forming a narrow and shallow channel, together with signs that, nearby, there had once existed a rectangular building. But the natural drop in the outfall of the lake could never have been enough to generate the power required by a mill, and it was made to drive the pumps in the Waterhouse only because of the artificial drop introduced by its being led under the building. No document mentions a mill in connection with the Manor of Kinnersley or The Old Farm, and Edward Carleton did not possess one within the precincts of Carshalton House. What Dr. Peatling saw may be evidence that the lake was at some time extended over land on which a building had once stood; but it is impossible now to say what that building was or what the purpose was of the shallow water channel.

Piped spring water for his house was not the only amenity that Sir John Fellowes obtained from his lakeside engineering. On the north and east of the pump room there was a bathroom with its adjoining dressing room. This again was luxury equipment at the time, even for a wealthy gentleman. (The name applied to it, Bagnio, indicates that the idea was an import from Italy – where, of course, it dated back to ancient Rome.) Sir John's bath was of marble, sunk in the ground and about ten feet square, with fine Dutch tiles lining the walls of the room in which it was installed and black and white marble squares beside the bath itself. In recent years this room has been adapted for use as a school dining room, and the bath has been floored over for even longer; but the early 18th century tiles remain on the walls, and it would not be very difficult to restore the original appearance of what is, like the Hermitage, a rare survival from the past. Removal of modern additions might also reveal, what is not now apparent but was probably the case, that there were means of heating the bath water. (A chimney over the room is otherwise inexplicable.)

Two items in Sir John's statement of expenditure seem to relate to his water engineering. £140 was paid to "George Devall, Plummer" and £110 to "Richard Cole, Engineer". The latter supplied a "water engine" for the estate of Robert Chester, another Director of the South Sea Company (who also employed Charles Bridgman to design his garden); while George Devall, by an odd coincidence, is known to have worked on the Radcliffe Observatory. £140 was a large sum of money in his time and it would have paid for a very extensive pipe-laying operation.

Adjoining the bath room, backing onto the pump room, and facing the lake there is a large chamber with an ornamental ceiling and, along its frontage, tall arched openings which have been made into windows but were, almost certainly, originally open, for this served as a garden lounge for the Fellowes household. And, finally completing the Waterhouse amenities, an orangery, again with tall arched openings, stretched for forty feet along the south side of the building, with a door at the east end leading to the pump room and stairs to the roof of the tower. The orangery had been intended for exotic plants in general, but, in his inventory, Sir John stated: "Memorandum. In the Greenhouse and Bagnio at the Bottom of the Garden there is neither Furniture nor Greens of any kind."

Except on one point there seems to have survived, in the late 19th century,

Early nineteenth century view by John Claude Nottes of the waterhouse and the pond at the mouth of West Street.

The Waterhouse and West Street from the south in the early nineteenth century.

The same scene viewed from the north. The seeming change in the façade of the Waterhouse is probably due to artistic licence. Neither in these two pictures nor in the one opposite does the back of the building correspond with its actual shape (see the plan on page 49).

no local knowledge of the history of the Waterhouse. At any rate, all that Bright-ling could say about it when, in 1872, he wrote his *History of Carshalton* was: "Respecting the building known as the Waterhouse, there appear to be no records. The ground floor, however, was an orangery." And, in fact, orange trees, carefully protected, were still growing there in Brightling's time — as is attested by a note in the *Peatling Papers* reporting the reminiscences of a workman engaged on repairs to the tower in the early 1870s.

The fact that the Waterhouse contained no chattels at all for entry in the 1721 inventory suggests that it was a very recent construction at that time. (Though lead pipes and a cistern in the tower were said by *The Philomena* in 1913 to bear the date 1717.) It has been thought that certain entries in Sir John's list of expenses may have related to the building of the Waterhouse. The two prin-cipal items in this category are the payment of £449. 4s. to "Hy Biggs, Carpenter" and of £456 to "Giles Dance, Mason". Significant, too, may be the payment of 20 guineas to "H. Joynes, Surveyor"; he was 'Comptroller' of the building of Blen-heim Palace until 1715, when he left to become 'Surveyor' of Kensington Palace. His association with Vanburgh at Blenheim, together with the Vanburgh-like architecture of the Waterhouse has led to the inference being drawn that Joynes designed the latter. For similar reasons he has also been credited with 'Wrencote' in Croydon. But the sum paid to him by Sir John Fellowes would not have covered a major commission, even in those days.

Giles Dance's son George designed the Mansion House, and a grandson George was the architect of Newgate Prison, but little is known of the achieve-ments of the old man himself — though it is on record that, in partnership with his son George, he did work costing £700 on South Sea House in 1726/7. Either a master mason or a master carpenter, in the 18th century, would have been pre-pared to undertake the construction of a building like the Waterhouse (hiring other tradesmen as required). But Biggs and Dance might have been employed on the stable block. The sad truth is, once again, that there is not sufficient evidence to justify any sure conclusion in the matter; and the architect of the Waterhouse is likely to remain for ever anonymous. (But Sir John evidently thought well of Henry Biggs, because he left him 10 guineas by his will.)

The compiler of the sale catalogue of 1839, waxing almost lyrical, described the Waterhouse as "a Spacious and lofty ivy-bound *[as it then was]* tower with wings, on the opposite side of the Water, forming a striking feature in the Views from the house, being handsomely designed and of an ornamental style of Archi-tecture, the Tower surmounted with Pinnacles, Stone Vases etc." And the building was not only an ornament to the grounds; it was part of the village land-scape. A writer in the *Gentleman's Magazine* in 1798 concluded a eulogy of the beauty of Carshalton with: "Looking to the west there is a number of pleasant houses, and, above dark foliage, rises the waterhouse, not unlike the tower of a church with pinnacles."

Carshalton as a whole—and West Street in particular— would indeed suffer a great diminution if they were to lose the Waterhouse. For the 'national heritage' and historical records it stands as an early eighteenth century architectural gem, the principal adornment of the "handsom Seat" created by the head of a pioneer government-backed commercial enterprise which collapsed in scandal and corruption.

CHAPTER SEVEN
Later eighteenth century owners

Edward Fellowes lived in Carshalton House for some six years after the death of Sir John, and then himself died on the 16th January 1731, aged 59. (The date 1730 on his memorial in Carshalton church belongs to the old calendar which ended the year at Lady Day – March 25th.) The younger brother left no will, so Coulson Fellowes, eldest son of William, the senior of the Fellowes brothers, inherited the old Carleton estate. He was already a substantial land-owner, and was evidently not interested in the Carshalton property, for he proceeded to sell it. The purchaser of the mansion and its grounds was the current Attorney General, Sir Philip Yorke. Some other parts of the estate were also bought by him; most of the rest went to Samuel Swinfen, who thereby added another item to his portfolio of land investments (a little later he was to acquire also the Manor of Rotherhithe).

The introduction of an Attorney General into the history of Carshalton House provided an odd coincidence: Charles I's Attorney General, Sir Edward Herbert, had at one time owned its predecessor, The Old Farm. But Sir Philip, unlike Sir Edward, was not a backer of lost causes. The Whig party had his enthusiastic support, and, not long after he had bought Carshalton House, he was appointed Lord Chief Justice of England. Harris's biography of him, published in 1847, describes the property purchase had had just made as "a handsome country residence, comprising a mansion and pleasure grounds at Carshalton near Croydon." And Harris goes on to say that "the journals of the day" expected the newly created peer to take the title of Baron of Carshalton. However, our Surrey village was not to be distinguished in that way. Sir Philip Yorke chose to become Baron of Hardwicke, an estate in Gloucestershire he had bought for £24,000 in 1725 as an investment.

Yorke's outstanding ability at the bar had very quickly made him wealthy and, all through his life, he continued to amass riches. By 1740 he seems to have felt that he needed something bigger than Hardwicke as a symbol of his financial status, for, in that year, he bought the bankrupt Earl of Oxford's Wimpole estate in Cambridgeshire. That same year he gave up his Carshalton property. His biographer says that, all the time, he had continued to reside mainly in Lincoln's Inn Fields, but Carshalton House had "formed a pleasant occasional retreat when his severe labours permitted this". He now had to go a lot further afield for a weekend in the country.

George Lord Anson.

Philip Earl of Hardwicke.

Two engraved portraits.
Left: Philip, Earl of Hardwicke. Right: George, Lord Anson.

Three years before he parted with Carshalton House, Lord Hardwicke had moved to the top of the legal hierarchy by resigning his Lord Chief Justiceship to become Lord Chancellor; and, later on, he was created Earl of Hardwicke. Throughout his career he continued to be active in Parliament, and he took a much more prominent role in party politics than would a modern Lord Chief Justice or Lord Chancellor. His most useful work, however, was done in the performance of the judicial duties of the latter office; during his tenure of it he formulated the principles which should govern the law of equity and made it much more certain in its operation. All the same, he was best known to the public as the sponsor of the Marriage Act of 1753, commonly called 'Lord Hardwicke's Act', which virtually put an end to clandestine marriages in England by making clergymen liable to transportation if they purported to join couples in holy wedlock without banns or licence.

There are no recorded activities of Lord Hardwicke at Carshalton House. And, apart from the already quoted mentions of it by his biographer, the latter's only other reference to it occurs in an account of a journey made by the Lord Chancellor to Portsmouth in August 1739. With three of his sons he set out from Carshalton early in the morning, stopped the night at Liphook, and reached his destination about noon the following day. After reviewing the warships there with full naval honours, the party went straight back to Carshalton, again breaking their journey for the night, and arriving home in the early afternoon. The only interest of this anecdote is the light it throws on journey times in the 18th century.

From what is recorded later it appears pretty certain that Carshalton House was bought from Lord Hardwicke in 1740 by William Mitchell of Hemingford in Huntingdonshire. According to a contemporary account, the latter's father, James Mitchell had been one of two brothers who came from Scotland to England "with packs on their backs; but by a most unheard of niggardliness and parsimony so raised their condition that they both died extremely rich." William Mitchell himself is described as "A short black man, rather inclinable to be fat and . . . thick set." His father, who died in 1728, had bought half the Manor of Hemingford, and this was inherited by William, the oldest surviving son. He was appointed Sheriff of the combined counties of Cambridgeshire and Huntingdonshire in 1737; and four years later he was elected M.P. for Huntingdonshire with the support of the Duke of Manchester, whose seat it had been before he succeeded to the dukedom. The election campaign nevertheless cost William Mitchell "a vast sum . . . in the Whig interest".

He made Carshalton House his principal residence, but "had a house at Hemingford Gray . . . where he was obliged sometimes to reside to keep up his interest in Huntingdonshire". His fellow member for the county was Coulson Fellowes, who, in 1737 had bought the Manor of Ramsey and earlier, after inheriting Carshalton House, had sold it to Lord Hardwicke when he was Sir Philip Yorke. I don't know whether or not people in those days said "It's a small world", or whether all this had anything to do with William Mitchell's coming to Carshalton.

Besides becoming the rated occupier of Carshalton House, he also insured it. Mr. Bernard Nurse found in the Guildhall Library a record of two insurance policies which were taken out by William Mitchell on the 20th June 1740 with the

Hand in Hand Insurance Company. The first of them covered "a Br. House vald. £1750. The Wash Hse, Brew Hse & Colonnade vald. £250, in a park on the West Side of the road at Carshalton near Banstead Downs in Surrey, his *[i.e. William Mitchell's]* Dwelling Hse." The second policy was for £700 on "a Build. ½ Br. ½ Timb. being Coach Houses, Stables and Barns and Wood House, belonging to his Dwelling Hse situate as aforesaid . . . and in his own possession." (The Wood House would, of course, have held the fuel used to heat the mansion; coal cellars at Carshalton House are not mentioned until the 19th century.)

The insurance documents are particularly interesting because they give the dimensions of the various buildings covered. The House was 80′ x 66′; the Colonnade 33′ x 14′; the Wash House 106′ x 13′; the Brew House 53′ x 8′; the Coach House 140′ x 21′; the Stables 40′ x 9′ and 40′ x 6′ (which seems uncomfortably narrow); the Barns 79′ x 22′ and 62′ x 22′; the Wood House 112′ x 20′; and a "Stable in the back yard" 28′ x 30′. These details enlarge our knowledge of Carshalton House as it once was; but the statement in the policy on the mansion that it contained "21 rooms wainscotted *[i.e. wood panelled]* " raises a problem. Does it mean that the lay-out of the ground floor was already the same as it is now, and there was no great hall occupying the centre of the building? An alternative possibility is that the hall counted as one room and the back kitchen as another, which, with the four Carleton/Fellowes parlours, and the kitchen, would make up the required number of rooms. The policy mentions "21 marble chimney pieces *[many of the closets had fireplaces]* , 1 portland do., and 1 large do. in ye Hall"; but the present entrance hall could hardly accommodate that. On the other hand, "ye Hall" is described as "right wainscot, paved with Marble Squares", and the present hall, though not wood panelled, *is* paved with black and white marble squares. However, a central great hall might have been similarly paved. Sir John Fellowes's statement of expenditure shows that he paid £110 to "John Mist, Pavior". But it must also be said that the bathroom in the Waterhouse was paved with black and white marble squares. Once again we have an item in the documentation of Carshalton House on whose interpretation there cannot be certainty. But having regard to the use Lord Hardwicke made of the place, and the comparatively short time he owned it, it seems very unlikely that he would have made any extensive alterations or additions to it.

The death of the "rather inclinable to be fat" William Mitchell at Carshalton on the 14th September 1745 was reported by the journals of the day, but no details of the event were given. The fact that he died intestate suggests that it was quite unexpected. Letters of administration were granted to his widow, Elizabeth (whose brother was the father of the three Gunning sisters, celebrated beauties of the 18th century). Elizabeth evidently liked Carshalton House, for she was its rated occupier for the next three years. Then, in April 1749, the assessment was taken over by William Mitchell, who was presumably the eldest son succeeding his mother after her decease. He seems, almost immediately, to have granted a three year lease of the premises to Lord Anson, because the latter was rated on them from November 1749 until 1752, during the second half of which latter year William Mitchell's name replaced his in the rate books.

Lord Anson had achieved fame, first, for a circumnavigation of the globe in difficult circumstances, and then for naval victories over the Spanish and French (which had earned him a barony). By 1749, however, he had an administrative post in the Admiralty and was shortly to become its First Lord. He had also been a Member of Parliament and was a political ally of Lord Hardwicke's. Undoubtedly it was that connection which, indirectly, led to Lord Anson's taking up residence in Carshalton. In 1748 he had married Elizabeth Yorke, the Lord Chancellor's elder daughter, and there is documentary evidence that she had fond memories of Carshalton House. (Probably Lord Hardwicke's family had spent more time in it than he had.) Some letters to her from her brother Joseph have been preserved among the Hardwicke papers in the British Library, and one, sent in June 1749, contains the following passage: "I wish you joy of Carshalton, which, I am sure, gives you great pleasure & I am persuaded Lord Anson will like it as much as you do when he comes to know the beauties of it. I shall be curious to know whether you fancied, as I did, that it looks a great deal less than when we lived there; the walks looked so narrow and so short, that I could not help laughing when I considered how immense I had formerly thought them . . ." (Who hasn't felt like that when revisiting places known in childhood?)

Joseph had evidently inspected Carshalton House before the Ansons took it over, for he also said in his June 1749 letter: "The Mitchells, entre nous, were but so many pigs, for I never saw a house kept in worse order in my life." (But whether or not that was fair criticism we have no means of knowing.)

A month later Lady Anson's brother was writing to her again, saying that a letter he had just received from her "diverted me most as it recalled to my mind all the scenes of my childhood in a comical light; & I enjoyed excessively the ideas which struck you upon inhabiting the same place, as mistress of it, where formerly one was constrained by the looks of Papa and Mamma. I daresay you were much surprised to find you could go out when you pleased & I question whether you had half the inclination to go out as you had then . . . . I long to be with you there, I assure you, but beg when I do go, that you would not lay me in the best bed-chamber but somewhere in the Gallery." (The significance of this request is not known; there was probably some family joke behind it.)

It appears from this letter that Lord Hardwicke, although notorious for the assiduity with which he sought sinecures for his five sons, had maintained strict discipline when they were young. Indeed, he evidently never ceased to behave patriarchally in his family, because, in March 1750, Joseph was writing to Lady Anson: "I like your distribution of the house at Carshalton; . . . I admire likewise your attention in making Papa think Carshalton was still his, but must beg at the same time, when I return there again, that you would not surprise me in the same manner, for I expect to have permission to go where I please, and that I may be permitted to break fishing rods if I please [as late as 1888 a sale catalogue stated: "The Lake is well stocked with Trout"] & gather damsons in the drying-ground, tho' you should look out of your dressing room window; these preliminaries agreed upon on your part I may one time or other pay you a visit, & hope the day I arrive that Neptune will (tho' I believe it is only Triton) welcome me with his jet d'eau. Did Sweeting teach the trouts to eat again, for of that you say nothing, for that was too pretty a thing to be neglected."

It is likely that Elizabeth took a keen interest in the garden of Carshalton House, for, according to Sir John Barrow's biography of Lord Anson, he and his wife were "fond of rural life and enjoyed the pleasure of floriculture and planting".

The water-spouting figure of Neptune (or Triton) mentioned in Joseph's letter may have been a part of the statuary for which Sir John Fellowes had paid Robert Hartshorne £149. 16s. It is not referred to by anyone else; but, by what was probably no chance coincidence, there was a similar statue on top of the grotto in Carshalton Park, for which Thomas Scawen was responsible. The two families seem to have vied with each other in what nowadays is called 'conspicuous expenditure'.

In 1751 Lord Anson bought Moor Park in Staffordshire, and that almost certainly accounts for the disappearance of his name from Carshalton's rate books. William Mitchell was once again the rated occupier of Carshalton House, remaining so until 1754. But it seems that his heart was really in Hemingford, for, in that year, he sold his Carshalton estate to George Amyand. The Mitchell family continued to hold the Manor of Hemingford right up to the end of the 19th century; and, in 1755, William Mitchell, like his father before him, was Sheriff of Huntingdonshire and Cambridgeshire. (My non-Carshalton information about the Mitchells comes from *The House of Commons 1715-1754* and the *Victoria County History of Huntingdonshire*.)

Most of the available information about George Amyand, the new owner of Carshalton House, is to be found in *The History of Parliament: The House of Commons 1754-1790*, edited by Sir Lewis Namier and John Brooke. George was the second son of Claudius Amyand, serjeant surgeon to George II, but he did not follow his father's profession. Instead, after the usual formal apprenticeship to a London merchant, he began trading on his own account, establishing commercial relationships particularly with merchants in Hamburg and marrying the daughter of one of them. Like a number of Carshalton House's owners, Amyand was as much a financier as a trader, and, in addition to his partnership in the firm of Amyand and Rucker, merchants, of Laurence Pountney Hill, he had a lucrative share in the banking firm of Amyand, Staples and Mercer. (Incidentally, John Anthony Rucker, his merchant partner, lived in Strawberry Lodge, Carshalton, and was later one of the executors of Amyand's will.)

In those days — and for long afterwards — prominent men in the City commonly sought to become legislators; and George Amyand was only following an established pattern when, in 1754, (the year of his acquisition of Carshalton House) he presented himself to the electors of Barnstaple as their future Member of Parliament. It was, of course, a carpet-bagging job. Amyand had the backing of political friends made through his elder brother who was already in Parliament; and "To defray all expenses exceeding £1500 *[most of which would have been for bribes to electors]* he received £2,000 from secret service funds." It followed that, after his election, he was a staunch supporter of the government of the day; and it followed, too, that he obtained a number of profitable government contracts.

In 1760, and again in 1763, Amyand was appointed a director of the East India Company; and, in 1764, he reached the high point of his career, when, like John Fellowes, he was given a baronetcy. Two years later he was dead, and his friend, Sir James Porter, was writing: "Sir George is no more. He has left clear £160,000 sterling and perhaps more. This pursuit, keen and arduous, worked the capillaries of his brain, wore them to a filament, distorted their whole construction, and dissolved the whole frame at 46." Although the language and medical notions of this belong to their age, in essence it might be the epitaph of some modern business-man who has failed to stand up to the physical and mental strains of making a fortune. A statement of Sir George Amyand's finances at his death shows that most of his £160,000 was in commercial enterprises, but an estate in Berkshire was valued at £30,000. (His Carshalton property figured at only £5,000, and his town house in Great George Street — which was leased — at a mere £3,300.)

When Sir George died, his youngest child was only five, and the family was soon to be doubly orphaned. Their mother was even shorter lived than her husband, dying in 1767 at the age of 42. A monumental urn in Carshalton church commemorates them both and adds the information that "to imitate their virtues and lament their deaths they left 2 sons and 2 daughters." The estate in Berkshire had been entailed by Sir George's will for the benefit of the elder son, George, and his male heirs. This was done, in the testator's words, "to annex to the Title an Estate Sufficient to Support the Dignity" (Sir George was clearly very proud of his baronetcy). But George, the son, when he married the heiress of Velters Cornewall of Moccas Court, Hereford, changed his name to Cornewall. So he inherited the Title and the Dignity and the Estate, but did not preserve his father's memory.

His mother had been given £3,000, an annuity of £300, all the household goods, and a life interest in both the town house and the Carshalton property (which latter is stated in the will to have been "purchased of William Mitchell, Esq."); £12,000 was left in trust for the younger son, John, but £10,000 of this was capital staying in the partnership of Amyand and Rucker, and John eventually went into that business. He prospered in it and was elected to Parliament in 1774 (in which year his elder brother became M.P. for Herefordshire). John died in 1780 and was buried in Carshalton churchyard, though the rate books do not show him as resident in the parish. His two sisters had been bequeathed £10,000 each by their father's will, the money to be paid when they attained the age of 21 or sooner married. No doubt this helped their subsequent marraiges to, respectively, the Earl of Malmesbury and the Earl of Minto.

Besides substantial legacies to his business partners and some of his kin, Sir George had left £150 to the East India Company for its Hospital in Poplar, £30 to "each of the Clerks in my Compting House" and £20 to "each of the Clerks in my Banking Shop". In addition, £100 was "to be distributed among my Menial Servants at the Discretion of my dear Wife." The residue of the estate went to George, and it was also noted in the will that the two boys would share about £41,000 from the estate of their Hamburg grandmother.

A deed in the Minet Library shows that, in 1760, Amyand had taken a 21 years' lease of the Carshalton land which Coulson Fellowes had sold to Samuel Swinfen. So, after the death of Dame Anna Maria Amyand, it was, to some extent, the original Carleton estate which was up for sale again. The purchaser this time was the Hon. Thomas Walpole, another City merchant with a seat in Parliament. He was the second son of Baron Walpole of Wolperton and nephew to the great Sir Robert Walpole. His political career began, however, not through that family connection, but as a result of his marriage to the daughter of Sir Joshua Vanneck, who was described, when he died, as "one of the richest merchants in Europe". (By coincidence, one of Amyand's partners was another son-in-law of Vanneck's.) The financial status Walpole acquired through his wife's father enabled him to spend enough money on bribes to win Sudbury in 1754 (the year in which Amyand was returned for Barnstaple). The Honourable Thomas already had a government contract to victual the garrison in Gibraltar, and, for a year prior to his becoming a Member of Parliament, he had been a director of the East India Company. Though he continued to be active in the affairs of that Company, he became more financially involved in a number of other business and commercial enterprises. He was a partner in the banking firm of Walpole and Ellison, and, together with his father-in-law, obtained a contract to supply tobacco to the French monopolists of that commodity. He also became deeply involved in a project to develop a large area of Ohio.

The official title of that last-mentioned enterprise was the Grand Ohio Company, but it was commonly known as the 'Walpole Company'. The Hon. Thomas had formed it, in 1769, in association with Samuel Wharton, with the object of buying 2,400,000 acres of land ceded to the Crown by the 'Six Nations' of American Indians after the defeat of the French in the Seven Years' War. But the Company eventually developed this idea into a proposal to acquire 20 million acres of the land in question which was to be recognised as a new colony, under royal government, with the name of 'Pittsylvania'. This was presumably a tribute to William Pitt the Elder, of whom Walpole was a great admirer; but the name was later changed to 'Vandalia', which seems likely to have been a tribute to the Wandle (in Latin, *Vandalis*), one source of which lay in the grounds of Carshalton House. If so, one of the 'might-have-beens' of history is that Carshalton supplied a name for one of the United States of America. The Company had, indeed, the backing of a number of influential people on both sides of the Atlantic – including Benjamin Franklin; and Treasury approval of the required royal grant was obtained. But there was considerable opposition to the whole enterprise from rival commercial interests, with the result that all the necessary consents had not been obtained before the outbreak of the War of American Independence – which eventually left the British Crown with no say at all in what was to happen in Ohio.

Naturally, Walpole's few interventions in House of Commons debates were all on commercial and financial matters, and he has left no mark on the political history of the period. But, as a representative of 'the City', he was not without influence in government circles. And, as was the custom of the time, he used his parliamentary position, at every opportunity, to further his own financial interests.

The purchase of Carshalton House followed on his giving up an estate in Hayes which he had bought in 1765 from William Pitt the Elder (who, the following year, was to be created Earl of Chatham). After the sale the vendor began to pine so much for his former home at Hayes that Lady Chatham told Walpole that her husband would not be restored to health unless he was allowed to re-purchase the property. Walpole protested that "Hayes is become part of myself. It is the support of my life and of that spirit which enables me to seek from an independent industry the advancement of my family." (Whether he subsequently came to feel the same about Carshalton House is not recorded.) But in the end, in spite of the fact that he was in the middle of re-building the Hayes mansion, he did sell it back to the Chathams. "No person but Lord Chatham and no situation but his could have induced me to take the part I have done," Walpole informed Lady Chatham.

It seems to have been an occupational risk run by owners of Carshalton

House that they should suffer financial disaster while residing there. At any rate, the Hon. Thomas Walpole was the third of them to end his stay in Carshalton with his fortune in ruins. His troubles began in 1772 when the failure of another banking firm caused a run on his own. Not long afterwards he lost the very valuable French tobacco contract. And then the outbreak of the American War of Independence removed all hope of profit from his financial ventures across the Atlantic. By 1780 he owed the Bank of England £160,000, and, in that year, he went to Paris to conduct some very complicated and prolonged litigation over forfeited securities for loans he had raised. He lived mainly in France for the next nine years, and, in 1782, Carshalton House was sold, together with his town house in Lincoln's Inn Fields.

While abroad Walpole attempted to use his knowledge of French affairs to get diplomatic employment in the tripartite negotiations which were taking place between France, the American colonists and England. But as, by now, he was on bad terms with his former associate, Benjamin Franklin, who was the colonists' delegate in Paris, the English government decided that it would be inadvisable to avail itself of Walpole's proferred services.

After lengthy haggling over his indebtedness to the Bank of England, he finally reached a settlement which salvaged something from his financial shipwreck; and, in 1789, with the French Revolution already in motion, he at last returned to England. Walpole lived on to reach his 76th birthday, dying at Chiswick in 1803; but, though not by any means a poor man — as his will shows — he never regained his former prosperity.

All the foregoing facts about his career have been obtained from the previously mentioned *History of Parliament: The House of Commons 1754-1790*. In local histories he gets mention only because his celebrated cousin, Horace Walpole, was visiting him when he wrote the tribute to Carshalton's rural charm which has been quoted by pretty well everybody who has ever written about the place. Occasional appearances of the Hon. Thomas Walpole's name in Carshalton Vestry's minute book show only that he took part in the affairs of the parish to the limited extent expected of an 18th century gentleman, but no more. In 1774, William Gilpin, the then headmaster of the well-known Cheam School (when it was at Cheam) wrote of Carshalton that there were "one or two houses worth visiting, particularly Mr. Walpole's which, a few years ago, belonged to Lord Anson." In fact, Lord Anson had given up Carshalton House twenty years previously, after having lived in it for only three years; but to Dr. Gilpin, who was evidently a bit of a snob, that was far more important than the much longer subsequent occupation of the premises by Sir George Amyand and Walpole himself. Yet the probability is that the Hon. Thomas had more to do with making the Carshalton House mansion what it is now than any other owner after its builder.

One result of the alterations to the premises for which I believe Walpole was responsible was the creation of what has become, in the opinion of many people, the most attractive room in the house. Variously called the Blue Room, the Italian Room and the Adam Room, this 'Parlour' has always constituted a puzzle. Assuming that the logical route was taken by the Carleton and Fellowes inventory makers, the room can be identified as the early 18th century 'Common Parlour' which had the old kitchen opposite it on the other side of the 'passage' corresponding to the present entrance hall. The *Victoria County History* described this

The Blue (or 'Adam') Room.

64

room as "most elaborately ornamented . . . with an Ionic arcading round its walls, having an entablature with a carved frieze." Mr. Derek Sherborn, in the *Country Life* article already quoted from, said that it was "a room showing striking originality in its rich Palladian decoration . . .". Pevsner and Nairn, in their *Buildings of Surrey*, while praising "the SW corner room" as, jointly with the Entrance Hall, "by far the finest in the house", were perplexed by it to the extent of enquiring "What was the purpose of this room?" They could only say that it was "in a very personal taste", and they dated it "probably of c.1720". But this seems far too early for a room which, by its style of decoration, attracted, quite plausibly, the description 'Adam'.

In the 1839 sale catalogue the room appeared as "Breakfast Room with alcove recess, furnished with Columns and Pilasters in Gray and White, Marble Chimney Piece etc., and a Dressing Closet or Studio adjoining". (This last was undoubtedly the plain 'Closet' of the early 18th century inventories.) By 1888, when the property was again up for auction, the room had somehow become an "Elegant Boudoir" (though, according to Charles Barrett, it was his father's study) with a "small Writing Cabinet adjoining with panelled walls" and an alcove recess 11′ 6″ x 9′.

The room is, indeed, a beautiful one, with heavily undercut carved wood ornamentation of, as Mr. Sherborn put it, "almost lace-like delicacy". Such work could have been produced at almost any time in the 18th century after Grinling Gibbons had shown the way. Charles Barrett asserted, in his notes: "As a matter of fact, the room was carved by an Italian craftsman who probably executed a good deal more of the work in the house. In the old parchment plans of the house it is always called the Italian Room." Nothing is now known about those plans, and Barrett's statement cannot be verified. But whatever craftsman worked on the room in question, the columns and pilasters, the colour scheme and, above all, the marble chimney piece suggest 'Robert Adam' in style. That does not mean that he designed this part of Carshalton House — though he did carry out a lot of work on 'The Oaks' nearby, for Lord Derby. The 'Adam' style was copied by a number of his contemporaries, and the period when his decorative effects were most fashionable coincided with the Hon. Thomas Walpole's tenure of Carshalton House.

But why should this room have been singled out to be decorated in a style which, in the opinion of experts, is unlike that of any other 'parlour' in the house? The answer, I suggest, is that the room had to be completely remodelled after its north-west corner had been cut off to allow the present 'service' staircase of the mansion to be constructed. The ground floor plan of the house (see page 43) shows clearly that this was how space was found for that staircase. But the main staircase, too, is in a cramped situation. Pevsner and Nairn called it "unaccountably small" and Mr. Sherborn said that it was "confined to a space of small dimensions, so that the fine craftsmanship of its well-turned balusters and carved brackets hardly shows to advantage".

Charles Barrett wrote: "The staircase of carved oak has unfortunately been spoilt by being shorn of one of its first two flights"; but he gave no authority for this statement, and it may have been merely an inference he drew from the fact that these stairs do not continue on to the second floor. There is, however, nothing in the Carleton and Fellowes inventories to suggest that the 'Great Stair Case' originally went on beyond the first floor. What, pretty certainly, did serve

Door furniture in the Blue (or 'Adam') Room.

the second floor was a small staircase which, in this century, until very recently, has run only from the basement to beside the Painted Parlour. (Space readily available above it has now enabled it to be carried to the top of the house in order to satisfy modern fire regulations.) In the Carleton inventory the room over the Painted Parlour is called "the furthest Roome on the Stairs"; and there exists on the ground floor at this spot the remains of old balustrading, the design of which corresponds with that of the second and third flights of the present 'servants' staircase. That, rising from the basement, serves all floors but it does not appear to have been constructed all at the same time; indeed, as has been said, on the ground floor, space seems to have been found for it only by taking away from the 'Adam' room its north west corner. From the basement to the ground floor the banisters of this staircase are of a plain, bulbous shape, without carving, but in the next two flights they are (allowing for some modern replacements) alternately twisted 'barley sugar' and fluted classical columns, with the newel posts also in the latter style.

The present main staircase — on the other side of the entrance hall — has fluted classical newel posts, but the banisters are all of the 'barley sugar' type. However, from the appearance of the underside of the carved handrail, and certain other indications, Sister Pauline Stevens is of the opinion that this staircase is actually a re-assembly of components which are not all in their original position.

What all this indicates is a matter for speculation — or bafflement. But one possible explanation is that the removal of a 'great staircase' from a central hall to permit the latter's division into two rooms, left an 'all floors' service staircase beside the Painted Parlour which no longer gave access to the entrance hall, and, along with the main staircase, had to be re-sited. The Carleton inventory indicates that there was already a service staircase "In the passage", because, between that entry and "In the Comon Parlour", comes "In the Closet at the Stairs Foot". The contents of this closet show it to have been more of a room than a cupboard, and space could hardly have been found for it at the foot of the present service staircase. But such a closet could have been accommodated beside a modest 'Carleton' service staircase which took up only part of the area now occupied by the present main one. And, later on, if the 'great staircase' was removed from a central hall, the most convenient place in which to construct its successor might well have been the site of the Carleton closet and back stairs. Space would then have had to be found for a replacement of the service staircase, and that would account for the 'Adam' room's having lost its north west corner. Ample materials to build the present main and service staircases could have been obtained from the dismantling of a 'great staircase' in the central hall and a staircase beside the Painted Parlour.

There are, however, conflicting opinions about the probable date of the elements of the present two staircases. The *Peatling Papers* include a letter from an expert mentioning other staircases, dated 1710-1720, which have banisters like those at Carshalton House. On the other hand, another expert pointed out that they are carved in the same way as those in the staircase of Beacon House, Painswick, which is dated to c.1769. It is never safe to rely entirely on these stylistic resemblances. Joiners worked from pattern books, and there was nothing to prevent a craftsman from using an old one, or a client from preferring its designs.

What is very difficult to believe is that the original designer of Carshalton House would have squeezed such an important feature of the house as the great staircase into so exiguous a compass and such an insignificant position as it now occupies in the mansion. Some very compelling reason must surely have presented itself, after the place had been built, to justify spoiling its harmonious composition in such a way. And the only reason I can think of is the removal of a former great staircase rising from a central hall, and the conversion of the latter into two rooms. (In this connection, it is noteworthy that the two rooms now in the centre of the house are divided only by a partition – not a load-bearing – wall, with folding doors.) But why should anyone want to remove the great staircase and divide up the original hall? When the *Victoria County History* was published early in this century, it said that "The principal entrance opened into a large panelled hall, now used as a library." And it may be that the Hon. Thomas Walpole, like a number of his contemporaries, wanted a 'Library' in his house. But that is only one of many guesses that might be made, and there is no way of being certain that any one of them is the truth. However, facts which all point to one conclusion still support that conclusion, even though the human motives involved are unknown.

And there are yet other facts pointing in the same direction. By the time the premises came to be described in the sale catalogue of 1839, the kitchen was no longer on the ground floor; it had been relegated to the basement. A kitchen opening onto the Entrance Hall of a mansion would undoubtedly have seemed to our ancestors a very strange juxtaposition of 'upstairs' and 'downstairs'; and it is extremely unlikely that Edward Carleton planned any such incongruity. Much more probably, what is now the Entrance Hall was originally the passage leading off the old great hall to the domestic offices; and, when its status was raised, the kitchen had to be banished to the nether regions.

The architecture of the present Entrance Hall led Pevsner and Nairn to date it "c.1750" and to bracket it with the 'Adam Room' as "by far the finest rooms" in the house. Mr. Derek Sherborn remarked that the decorative features of the 'Blue Parlour' (as the 'Adam Room' was alternatively called) "repeat in a more elaborate form and on a smaller scale those found in the vaulted hall (*which, Sister Pauline Stevens noted, has, very significantly, the remains of a plain, flat ceiling behind the vaulting*), and it is evident that both were designed by the same man." Going by similarities in their features to those in Asgill House, Richmond, which was designed by Sir Robert Taylor and completed in 1767, Mr. Sherborn suggested that this architect was commissioned also to carry out work in Carshalton House. The Hon. Thomas Walpole had moved into the mansion in 1767, but Mr. Sherborn does not seem to have been aware of this, for he named Lord Hardwicke, "who died in 1764", or "his successor, Thomas *[sic]* Broadhead" as possible employers of Sir Robert Taylor. In fact, Lord Hardwicke had parted with Carshalton House 24 years before he died, and Theodore Broadhead did not buy it until 1782. That, of course, does not disprove the suggestion that Sir Robert Taylor was responsible for the decoration of the 'Adam Room' and the present Entrance Hall (though it would have been a small commission for an architect of sufficient calibre to be engaged, as Sir Robert Taylor was, to do work on the Bank of England). Mr. Sherborn thought that the rococo ceiling and marble fireplace in the Oak Room, together with the pedimented and pillared porch on the south front, were also added at the same time; and it must be said that the fireplace in question is very similar to one in Asgill House (but that may only mean that the same craftsman executed both.)

All told, it seems unlikely that the identity of the architect of all these 'modernisations' in Carshalton House will ever be established with certainty. But whoever he was, the owner most likely to have employed him was the Hon. Thomas Walpole. After all, he had shown by his treatment of the home of William Pitt the Elder that he was quite prepared to set about reconstructing a mansion.

In 1782, while Walpole was in France, Carshalton House was bought by Theodore Henry Broadhead, about whom all that I have been able to discover comes from the *Gentleman's Magazine* which, after announcing his death on the 20th April 1810 at Portland Place, "aged about 74", continued: "His name was originally Brinkwood and his father was a native of Holland. He took the name of Broadwood *[sic]* at the desire of his maternal uncle of that name, who left him a very considerable fortune." That may have left him with no need to earn a living; certainly no occupation is assigned to him in any document. But in 1786 he was Sheriff of Surrey, an appointment which required high social and financial status. The Court Rolls of the Carshalton manor, when recording the transfer of the 'Swan Inn' from Walpole to Broadhead, show also that the latter had a town residence in Portland Place.

Charles Barrett, the enthusiastic but very opiniated late 19th century owner-historian of Carshalton House, manifested in his notes a strong dislike of Theodore Broadhead. This was because Barrett believed that Broadhead was responsible for a major alteration to the original mansion. That belief, unfortunately, was founded on two misconceptions: one, that Sir John Fellowes had built Carshalton House; and the other, that, to quote from Barrett's *Surrey: Highways, Byways and Waterways*: "In the Painted Room at Carshalton House there is still a panel which assuredly represents Fellowes' House, though the background is decidedly fanciful." This idea of Barrett's was actually as fanciful as the background. The picture in question is in rather a different style from those on the rest of the wall space. It depicts a white-coloured house at the end of a long avenue in which men and women in early 18th century costume are strolling and chatting. One of the ladies has a black servant — a fashionable kind of attendant in Sir John Fellowes's time. In the foreground of the avenue stands an extravagantly baroque fountain much cluttered with statuary. Charles Barrett considered this to be evidence that the scene represented Carshalton House as it once was, because "on the front lawn during dry seasons traces appear of a large circle and in the picture a large circular fountain appears. Moreover, too, the leaden water-pipes take, on both sides, the direction of this circular space." But, if there *was* formerly a fountain in front of the mansion, could it not have been the water-spouting figure of Neptune (or Triton) — on a circular base — which Joseph Yorke had hoped would welcome him on his arrival at what was then his sister's home?

The house in the picture has a roof topped by a cupola and balustrading which belong in style to the reign of Charles II. The opinion of Mr. Derek Sherborn was that "if not an imaginary scene *[it]* may have been based on an engraving of some Dutch building". And, when I asked the National Trust whether they could identify the house, their experts thought it had a continental look. However that may be, there is one obvious reason why the house in the picture could not be Carshalton House: its frontage exhibits two rows of twelve windows where the present mansion has only nine windows on each floor. Even if it had

Wall painting in the Painted Parlour, probably of an imaginary house and garden.

been possible to effect the required transformation of the façade, signs of alteration to the brickwork could not have been avoided; but it is plainly all still in its original state.

Amazingly, Barrett does not seem to have noticed these facts. He never referred to the main windows of the mansion when he wrote in his book: "Fellowes built a house consisting of a basement, ground floor and first floor. In the high roof were dormers, the top was balustraded and there was a glazed cupola." The Fellowes' inventory shows clearly that the house already had three floors above the basement, and what Barrett seems to be describing is the picture in the Painted Parlour, which exhibits all the features he mentioned, except for the dormers.

Citing no other authority but his theory about the painted house, Barrett went on to assert that Theodore Broadhead removed the roof and the cupola, and then added the present top storey of Carshalton House. But the accommodation on the top floor is exactly the same now as it was when the Carleton and Fellowes inventories were made. On the other hand, it must be said that the brickwork of the attic storey is, on the south side of the building – thought not on the north and east sides – a shade darker in colour than that lower down. Plenty of explanations could be thought up to account for that. It is more difficult, however, to account for the first item in the Carleton inventory, which was: "On the Leads: a speaking Trumpet and two turkey Work Chairs". Those articles could not conceivably have been in the open on the roof. In what sense, then, should "On the Leads" be interpreted? Could the expression have possibly meant a glazed cupola? Did Edward Carleton loll at ease in a turkey work chair on top of his mansion while broadcasting orders to the gardeners through an early form of megaphone? There is no corresponding entry in the Fellowes inventory to help answer those questions. And nobody now knows anything about the old parchment plans of the mansion, spoken of by Barrett; so it is impossible to say whether he got the top storey dormer windows from those, or from his imagination, or from some source he never mentioned.

A recent, non-documentary, discovery provides strong evidence that, at some time, an alteration was indeed made to the external appearance of the roof. Repair work revealed, at the end of the side walls of attic bedrooms, a roughly triangular, brick in-filling, pointing downwards and carrying the upper part of the wall up to the exterior wall. This suggests that the roof originally had a different slope which did not meet the exterior wall as it is now. Beyond that is guess-work. No date can be put on the in-filling; but the Hon. Thomas Walpole is more likely to have been responsible for it than Theodore Broadhead. (The 'Watts' engraving, dated only a year after Broadhead acquired the premises, shows the top storey just as it is now). Incidentally, the new discovery might explain the present undue prominence of the cornice; it may have looked very different under the roof designed by the original builder.

Incidentally, Charles Barrett's conviction that the original Carshalton House was depicted in the Painted Parlour led him to conclude that the carriage drive once "went straight down to the house through the middle of the field and parallel to the drive to-day"; and he asserted that "about fifteen or twenty years since *[i.e. 1875-1880]* the drain gullies were discovered. The depression in this field still marks the line of the old roadway." But Sister Pauline Stevens has pointed out that it might, in fact, mark the line of the ancient public right of way which ran through the present grounds of Carshalton House in the 17th century.

In 1792, for reasons unknown, Theodore Broadhead sold his Carshalton estate to John Hodson Durand. Manning and Bray's history of Surrey, published at about this time, shows that mis-statements concerning even contemporary events may be found in the most carefully compiled historical work. The two learned authors named the Hon. Thomas Walpole as the vendor to Durand. Brightling, relying, by his own account, on the best authorities, erred much more grievously. He wrote: "In 1792 it [Carshalton House] was the property of Theodore Broadhead, then of the Honourable Thomas Walpole." Fortunately, the land deeds in the Surrey Record Office provide an unquestionable record of the sequence of owners.

John Hodson Durand and his siblings formed a most extraordinary household. His father was John Durand, about whom it can be learned from the previously mentioned *History of the House of Commons* that he was a ship's captain in the East India Company's service before setting up on his own account as a merchant. His address is given in 18th century London directories as 51, Lime Street, and there he prospered exceedingly. He served a term as Sheriff of Surrey in 1767, and he was also appointed an Elder Brother of Trinity House and Director of Greenwich Hospital. Eventually he became wealthy enough (at a time when parliamentary elections could still be won by bribery) to gain a foothold in the House of Commons. He represented successively Aylesbury, Plympton and Seaford; there duly followed government contracts for victualling troops, providing masts for the navy, and supplying materials needed in the war against the rebel American colonists. In 1780 the *English Chronicle* wrote of him: "No man understands the *Multiplication Table* with more comprehensiveness and precision of intelligence; but in the laws of his country, or in the duties of a legislator, there is perhaps no individual more completely ignorant." That, however, was the view of a journal on the other side politically.

John Durand died on the 19th July 1788, aged 69, and his will was proved twelve days later. He left a life interest in all his freehold property to John Hodson Durand, after whose death the latter's eldest surviving son was to inherit it absolutely. If there was no surviving son or grandson of John Hodson Durand the property was to go, in order of seniority, to whichever of Matthew Durand, Anne Durand, Elizabeth Durand, Charlotte Durand, Jane Durand and Sarah Durand could provide the necessary male heir. There was nothing very unusual in these provisions; what was extraordinary was that all these Durands, including John Hodson, were described as "my natural or reputed son/daughter". In old wills "natural" does not necessarily mean illegitimate; but John Durand permitted no doubt about the matter, because one of his bequests was an annuity of £20 to "Elizabeth Stacey, now of Epsom, Single woman (the Mother of my said natural or reputed Daughter Charlotte Durand)". £20 a year would have been as much as a labourer earned in those days, so the bequest guaranteed Miss Stacey against destitution for the rest of her life. Three other women were also left an annuity of £20 in the same part of the will. They were "Elizabeth, wife of Richard Pearce, now of Ewell, ffarmer", "Jane Hall, the wife of Robert Hall, now of Beddington, Husbandman" and "Jane Divall, wife of Richard Divall, now of Walton, Surrey, late my Huntsman". One cannot help wondering, in the circumstances, whether these ladies had also contributed illegitimate offspring to John Durand's collection,

72

but he had refrained from making this explicit to save the feelings of their husbands. (Mrs. Naseer, "formerly my housekeeper in Bengal and now residing at Calcutta" got only a straight £10, so it can be assumed that she had borne her employer no child.)

John Hodson Durand was clearly the favourite son — though he had been expected to earn his living. (When the will was made, in 1785, he was "second mate of the Contractor, East India ship".) He was bequeathed outright all his father's copyholds and leaseholds, together with £12,000 in cash and the residue of the estate after all the legacies had been provided for. Matthew was given "the perpetual advowson of Breeden in the County of Worcester", and £12,000 was put in trust to go to him when he attained the age of 25 or married, whichever event occurred first. (John Durand was evidently a believer in marriage for other people.) £10,000 was also left in trust for each of Anne and Elizabeth to provide them with an income for life, and, after their death, the money was to be divided equally among their children (providing those were legitimate). These two daughters are stated in the will to be living with their father in his "house in Carshalton". The other three daughters were all at "Messrs. Ray and ffry's Boarding School at Streatham", and they had £10,000 put in trust to give each a dowry of £2,000 on marriage under the age of 45 with the consent of the trustees of the will; in the meantime, they were to share the interest on the money.

But these seven Durand children did not constitute the whole of their father's illegitimate progeny. Another annuity of £20 went to "my natural or reputed son John Durand, late commander of the Northington, East Indian ship" (who literally complicates the issue very considerably). This John Durand was also forgiven £12,000, "part of the principal sum of £23,256. 3s. 8d. which he now owes me upon Bond". From this one might deduce that he was an eldest son who had upset his father over money. But I know of no reason why no testamentary recognition at all was given to "James, natural son of John Durand Esq. and Jane Matthews", whose baptism on the 30th July 1775 is on record in the Carshalton parish registers.

At the end of his will, the old man recommended "all my children to live in peace and amity with each other"; but whether they did is not recorded. In fact, nothing is known about any of them, save John Hodson Durand (who, in his own will spelled his middle name 'Hodsdon'). One enigmatic provision of his father's will had left him £500 to hold in trust for payment to Martha Hassell, "now *[1785]* residing at Mrs. Prebble's School at Croydon", when she either married or became 21; and the testator concluded this bequest with "I recommend the said Martha Hassel to the Protection and Patronage of my said Son, John Hodson Durand." She was actually Martha Ann Hassel(l), and the Beddington parish registers record the baptism of "Marthar *[sic]* Ann, the base born child of Mary Hassel" on the 12th April 1772. What Martha Ann meant to John Durand is not known, but John Hods(d)on Durand married her on the 25th August 1788, barely six weeks after the old reprobate's death. Whether or not his philoprogenitive proclivities had led two of his offspring to contract unwittingly an incestuous marriage is a question to which no certain answer can ever be returned. But, in fairness to him, it must be said that, if he had not shown a sense of responsibility for the consequences of his behaviour, nothing would have been on record to blemish his respectability.

John Hods(d)on Durand could very accurately be described as 'a lucky bastard'. He was now a rich man, well able to afford to buy Carshalton House, as he did, for £9,765. And his financial – and, consequently, social – eminence was officially recognised when, in 1793, like his father before him, he was appointed Sheriff of Surrey. It appears, though, that he was not so good at holding on to a fortune as his sire had been at making one. At any rate, the shares in the East India Company which the son had inherited ceased to be registered in his name after 1802, while, three years previously, he had sold Carshalton House and returned to his former home, Woodcote Lodge. Whether these changes had anything to do with the expenses he incurred in connection with his election as M.P. for Maidstone in 1802 is a matter for conjecture. But it is a fact, as Sister Pauline Stevens established, that John Hods(d)on Durand later left Woodcote Lodge, and, after living for a time in Sutton, died in Kennington in 1830. Evidently he had continued to regard himself as a native of Carshalton, for he was buried in its churchyard – as had also been his eldest son, John Hassell Durand, who had predeceased him in 1824, and another son, Charles, born in 1797, who lived only three weeks. (George Bartlett Durand had been buried in Beddington churchyard, aged 16 months, in 1795.)

The will of "John Hodsdon Durand", made in 1827, describes him as "late of Woodcote Lodge and now of Sutton", but no house in that latter parish is named. From the bequests made, it appears that his wealth was now largely in the form of holdings of government stocks. Of these, enough was to be put in trust to provide incomes for life of £400 a year in the case of his two daughters, Mary Ann (the wife of Thomas Deacon "now residing in the East Indies") and Elizabeth (the wife of John Goodall), and £250 a year for his daughter Caroline (the wife of William Matthews). After their deaths, the capital sums involved were to be divided respectively among their children. For some reason not disclosed, the surviving son James was not in his father's favour, for he got an annuity of £100 only, and there was no provision that his children should inherit the capital after his death.

The will continues: "And whereas upon my separation with my wife Martha Ann Durand I settled and invested certain stock . . . in favour of my said wife . . .", and she gets a legacy of £500 only. The separation of the couple is probably explained by the bequest to "Clara Warren, Spinster, now residing in my house" of the income from £6,666. 13s. 4d. invested in 3% consolidated Bank annuities (i.e. £200 a year). She was also to receive the "Silver Tea Urn formed of the cup won by my horse Guildford at Oxford Races", and "a Silver Tankard formerly given to me by the said Clara Warren". But another silver cup won at Ascot by another of his horses went to John Roots who was one of the executors of the will and is described in it as "of Cotesford, Oxfordshire, Yeoman" (? also a racehorse trainer).

£100 was left by Durand to each of Christ's, the Bridewell and 'Bethlem' Hospitals; £10 "for Mourning" to each of his servants; and £200 to each of the three executors of his will. All the rest of his property – including a "sailing yacht" and gold cups (? sporting trophies) – he ordered to be sold and the proceeds invested in government stocks, the income from which was to be divided equally between his three daughters, with the capital going to their respective children after their decease.

There was a very informal sort of codicil which simply stated: "I direct that my Executors do purchase an annuity of £50 per annum for my Servant, Charlotte Maria Hart"; and, before probate was granted, this had to be explained by sworn statements from Edward Wallace (the current practitioner in the Carshalton family of surgeons), John Grace (landlord of the 'Greyhound' in Sutton), Mary Weight (a nurse and the wife of George Weight of Carshalton), William Matthews of Kennington (the testator's son-in-law) and Caroline Matthews (his daughter). They all deposed that they knew John Hodsdon Durand well, that he had become very infirm during the latter years of his life, "requiring continual care and assistance", and that, in consequence, Clara Warren had been employed "to be constantly with him and to act as his housekeeper". But she had died in 1828 (a year after the will was made) and Charlotte Maria Hart was engaged to take her place, remaining in the testator's service until his death (which happened in Kennington, presumably because he was then staying with the Matthews). The deponents further stated that Miss Hart "gave her whole time" to her employer, "who was in such an infirm state as to require assistance in dressing himself".

But it was Edward Wallace alone who could give the story of the codicil. On the 4th February 1830 he was with Durand "as his Medical Attendant", together with Mary Weight, the nurse, "in a room of the Inn called the Grey Hound at Sutton" where the invalid had been staying for about three weeks, accompanied by William and Caroline Matthews. The sick man remarked to his doctor (who was also one of the executors of the will) that he would like to do something for "that young girl", meaning Charlotte Maria Hart. But, when Wallace asked what he wanted to do, he refused to say until Mary Weight and the Matthews couple had left the room. He then told the doctor that he wanted the girl to have £50 a year; and to Wallace's suggestion that an annuity should be bought, he agreed that "that would be the best way". Wallace thereupon drew up the codicil on a sheet of paper, and, at Durand's instance, John Grace, the landlord of the 'Greyhound' (who had been a witness to the will), was fetched to join the doctor as a witness also to the codicil. Wallace then guided the testator's hand to make his mark, "he being too infirm to write"; and the codicil was later placed with the will by Durand himself.

Probate was granted, after these sworn statements had been considered, on the 3rd April 1830. Durand had died, aged 69, on the 28th February, but he was not buried until the 8th March, perhaps because of some difficulty over his being accepted as a Carshalton parishioner. Whether the Matthews moved from Kennington is not known, but Caroline Durand Matthews, aged 14, joined her grandfather in Carshalton churchyard in 1839.

All that now remains to preserve a memory of the family is a Wedgwood bowl, presented to Carshalton Cricket Club in 1796 and bearing, as well as that date, the initials "J.D.". This trophy was kept at Carshalton's 'Greyhound' where the Club held its annual dinners, but, eventually, an unpaid bill for those celebrations led to the bowl's seizure by the landlady. The sole source of this information is the already mentioned book by Charles Barrett. In it he goes on to say that the bowl "descended to a connection of the landlady, an old parish clerk of Carshalton named Waite or Wayte, by whom, just before his death, it was given away". (The Census returns for 1861 show that the parish clerk was actually John Weight, then aged 69.) Barrett does not name the donee of the bowl, but he showed that

The Carshalton Cricket Club's Wedgwood bowl dated 1796.
The lower picture shows the inside of the bowl, on the bottom.

he had had access to it by printing, in his book, a drawing he had made of it. A local newspaper said in 1934 that "in 1860 it passed into the possession of Dr. Barrett" (Charles's father; but he had not then come to live in Carshalton). This account continues: "Mr. Piers *[who lived in 'Queen's Well']*, hearing that Mr. Barrett *[Charles]* was leaving the house *[Carshalton House]*, called on him and was told that the bowl was still in existence and was being put up at Sotheby's for sale by auction." But Charles Barrett left Carshalton House round about 1888, and the bowl was not auctioned at Sotheby's until the 24th July 1909. It was bought by Mr. Piers for £29. 2s. 6d. and £35 was raised by public subscription to cover this sum and also provide a case for the bowl. It was then presented to the Carshalton Urban District Council for safe-keeping, and has since passed, of course, into the possession of the London Borough of Sutton. One can safely say that, if ever there is a Borough Museum, the bowl will be the rarest and most valuable exhibit in it. This specimen of 18th century Wedgwood ware cannot be other than absolutely unique, having regard to the inscription on it; and it has also the attraction of being decorated with a representation of a contemporary cricket match.

When the bowl was local news in this century, reference was made to Mr. Durand's continued concern for the parish of Carshalton although, at the time of the gift to the Cricket Club, he was living "so far from the centre of the village". This is odd, because, in 1796, John Hods(d)on Durand was still the rated occupier and owner of Carshalton House. There is actually no surviving evidence, apart from Charles Barrett's assertions, that J.H.D. had anything to do with the bowl. The initials on it are not exactly his, and, though his father died in 1788 and could not have been its donor, he had a "natural or reputed" step-brother named John Durand. Sister Pauline Stevens's researches also unearthed (not literally, of course) another John Durand who lived in Woodcote and died in 1834 at the age of 55. Where he came in the family tree it has been impossible to discover. He would have been only 17 when the bowl came into existence, but he could have been, on his age, a son of the John Durand who seems to have been the oldest illegitimate son of John Durand senior.

Once again, as so often in matters of local history (and, indeed, of national history), there is an element of uncertainty about the interpretation of facts. But John Durand as the donor of the Carshalton Cricket Club's bowl is a very shadowy figure if 'Hodson' — or 'Hodsdon' — is not inserted in his name. It would be a pity if such a splendid memento should really be associated with an unknown. And, at least, there is ample evidence in J.H.D.'s will that he was an enthusiastic sportsman.

CHAPTER EIGHT

A home becomes a school

There is nothing much to tell about the first two 19th century occupiers of Carshalton House. David Mitchell, who bought it from John Hods(d)on Durand in 1799, belonged to the same social class as its builder and a number of its subsequent owners. Manning and Bray describe him as a "Merchant" and his will gave his address as "the City of London". According to Dr. Peatling's notes he came from a Perthshire family, but his will mentions a brother living in Fifeshire. However, he undoubtedly was a Scot; he bequeathed £100 per annum for distribution among his poor relations in Scotland "who have been accustomed to have assistance from me". The *Gentleman's Magazine* announced his death on the 10th December 1804 at Bath (where, perhaps, he had gone to recover his health). He is referred to in the announcement as "of John Street, Bedford Row, London and Carshalton-house, Surrey", and this is the earliest reference to the present name of the mansion that I have come across. Thereafter it continued consistently to be called Carshalton House, but it would not be safe to conclude that David Mitchell was its godfather. In the 18th century houses were commonly identified by the name of their owner or occupier, and the premises themselves often remained anonymous.

When, in 1726/7, the Italian architect Leoni published plans for a "palace" which Thomas Scawen proposed to have erected in Carshalton Park, he named it "Carshalton House". But it turned out to be a castle in Spain, never actually being built; and, as the existing house in Carshalton Park was called 'Mascalls', 'Carshalton House' became a name available for use by any property owner who liked the sound of it. Incidentally, Leoni's appropriation of the name was probably responsible for some later misconceptions, including the statement in the *Victoria County History* that he designed the present Carshalton House, but that it has since been deprived of all its architectural ornament. The author of this assertion really ought to have noticed though, that, quite apart from architectural ornament, Leoni's drawings bear no resemblance at all to what we now see on the site.

From David Mitchell's will it is evident that his main commercial interests had been in Jamaica, where two of his brothers still were. He left the bulk of his estate in trust to them for the benefit of his infant sons, and Carshalton House was sold in 1805. The buyer was Clement Kynnersley of Sutton Hall, Derbyshire — which was still given as his address when he made his will in 1815, though he was then the rated occupier of Carshalton House. He evidently liked Carshalton, because he had owned 'Stone Court' for a few years prior to 1800, when it was sold and pulled down.

The Napoleonic Wars were having the customary effect on prices of all wars and Carshalton House cost Kynnersley £12,500. But he was given until 1808 to pay the first £6,500 and then allowed to settle the balance by instalments. The final payment of £2,000 was not made until 1813, and two years later the new owner died. He had married the daughter of Sir Wolstan Dixie of Bosworth Park, Leicestershire, but the couple had no children. Clement Kynnersley's will therefore left all his property to his nephew, Thomas Sneyd of Loxley Park, Staffordshire, "provided he do take the surname and use the arms of Kynnersley". It might be thought from this that the testator had bought Carshalton House because of its association with the Manor of Kinnersley; but there was nothing in the title deeds of the house about that ancient history, and it had long passed from the knowledge of all save dedicated students of medieval documents. In fact, the Kynnersleys in whom Clement took pride traced their origins to Herefordshire, where they owned a castle; they afterwards moved to Gloucestershire and, finally, the main branch settled in Loxley, Staffordshire. Clement Kynnersley actually owned Loxley Park where Thomas Sneyd was living, and the uncle's bequest made it well worth the nephew's while to change his name to Sneyd-Kynnersley. But he had been directed in the will to sell the Carshalton property in case the testator's other assets proved insufficient to pay his debts.

Carshalton House and the land which went with it now passed to William Foster Reynolds, but a slump in the value of real estate seems to have taken place after the peace brought by the Battle of Waterloo, for the price paid in 1815 was only £8,500, plus £500 for certain fittings. The mansion was once again the home of a member of the merchant class, although William Foster Reynolds does not seem, himself, to have been actively engaged in commerce. He was the eldest son of Foster Reynolds, a Quaker who, in the late 18th century, built up in 'The Culvers' a large bleaching "manufactory" — as it was called, though it actually depended entirely on sunlight and the clear waters of the Carshalton Wandle. After Foster Reynolds's death in 1798 his two younger sons, Thomas and Jacob Foster carried on the business, but William Foster seems to have inherited enough wealth to live without working. As was customary with Quakers, he had married a co-religionist, Esther Morris, who, herself, was related to two other well-known — and wealthy — Quaker families, the Frys and the Gurneys. William Foster Reynolds was wealthy enough himself to buy, as a land investment, the 'Long' estate (bounded by North Street, Mill Lane and Strawberry Lane) when it was for sale in the early 1820s following the demolition of the mansion which went with it. I have found nothing else recorded about his activities.

Brightling says that Reynolds "removed" from Carshalton House in 1840 and sold it; but the information given in Brightling's history of Carshalton is not always accurate, even when it relates to what was, for him, the quite recent past. Actually, as a notice in the *Gentleman's Magazine* informed readers, William Foster Reynolds died on the 19th November 1838, aged 70, and it was his executors who sold Carshalton House. In the Surrey Record Office at Kingston there is a copy of the 1839 sale catalogue and this has a historical interest its compilers count not have foreseen, for it gives a detailed and revealing account of the contemporary state of the "very Capital Handsome and Truly Comfortable Mansion in most Substantial Repair with Superior Offices of every Description". (The language of estate agents has not changed much in the meantime.) Improved travelling conditions had brought Carshalton House within handy reach of London, and the auctioneers made a point of the fact that it lay "only one mile from the Brighton Road at Sutton *[the fast, turnpike road]*; and only 10 miles from the several Bridges" (at that time, London, Blackfriars, Southwark, Waterloo, Westminster and Vauxhall).

From the further particulars given in the sale catalogue it becomes clear that some changes had been made since Sir John Fellowes's time. The top floor now had "a Housemaid's Closet and Washing ditto, with cistern, water and marble floor". More modern ideas of sanitation had also manifested themselves on the first floor where 'Water Closets' had been installed. But that floor still had its full complement of "Seven Bedrooms of very Superior Description, all lofty, cheerful and most of them furnished with Marble Chimney Pieces" – though one of them had now become a "Nursery with bath and a Closet with water laid on". On the other hand, the specifications of another of the main bedrooms contained an odd echo of the Carleton and Fellowes inventories; it was "decorated with well-selected Prints".

On the ground floor, the Painted Parlour was, in 1839, described as "a gentleman's room or study adapted for a Bedroom . . . with a Dressing-Closet with water laid on, and a separate Flight of Stone Stairs to the offices *[in the basement]* particularly convenient as connecting them with the Dining Room *[the Oak Room]*". It looks from this as if William Foster Reynolds had been a sick man for some time, largely confined to one downstairs room. (And perhaps he chose this one because the wall paintings gave an invalid something interesting to look at.)

The old ground floor kitchen and back kitchen are replaced in 1839 by "A Housekeeper's Room most conveniently fitted up with Closet Presses; a Butler's Room with Iron Plate-Closet and Water laid on", together with "a Bedroom above, a Lumber room or Store Closet, and back Entrance". Significantly, too, there is now no mention of a fireplace in the hall.

In the basement were "Servants' Hall with Shoe and Knife rooms adjoining; a Capital Kitchen with water; a Scullery & Bakehouse; Capital Larder; Cook's Pantry etc." (These rooms, Sister Pauline Stevens has established, ran in sequence from the south west to the north east, and the Pantry had an early Victorian lift which could have helped the Reynolds' family to get its meals piping hot.) There were also in the basement "large Coal Cellars" and "very capacious and excellent Cellars completely fitted up for Wine, Ale etc. with Bottle racks" (which latter are just what Sir John Fellowes had). "The whole *[is]* rendered dry and airy by a wide Area in which there is a Pump", adds the catalogue; and, after that, it was really superfluous to state that the house was "Elevated by a Flight of Stone Steps at each front, rendering it remarkably dry and healthy". But oddly enough, in the early part of this century, the basement was periodically flooded in wet seasons.)

The range of buildings to the west of the Colonnade still, in 1839, contained a Brewhouse, Wash-house and Dairy, while the "Ornamental Dove-House and Basins with an ample Supply of Water with Fountains etc." also probably dated back to the early 18th century. The gardens, however, seem to have undergone much development. In 1839 there were "Capital kitchen Gardens, inclosed and intersected by High Walls clothed with the choicest Fruit Trees; gravelled Walks and Flower gardens. 2 Hot Houses, 60 and 42 feet long . . . Vines and a Melon ground." In fact, the cultivated area was now so extensive that the auctioneers felt it advisable to point out that "Part of the Gardens, if considered too large, may be immediately appropriated to an Orchard or for the growth of common Root and Green crops." To the gentleman-owner it would have mattered little how common the crops were, because "the Farm Buildings and Gardens are completely screened from the Mansion."

The separate stable block for which Sir John Fellowes had probably been responsible was, of course, some distance from the house. In the yard behind it, which opened onto Shorts Road (then called Dark Lane), stood "Conveniently near the back gates a double cottage [each half having three rooms and a wash-house] for bailiff and gardener"; while, grouped round the same yard, were a "Carpenter's Workshop, Store Houses, Dog-Kennels & Boiling House". And the tally of domestic and agricultural amenities was completed by "a Drying ground, a Rickyard and small Paddock or Orchard with Sheep pens, a Cart lodge, a Turkey-house, a Pig yard and Piggery". There was also mention of an Ice-pit, unfortunately without its location being specified; it could well have dated back to the Carleton/Fellowes era, for that early equivalent of a modern 'deep-freeze' was already then commonly found in the grounds of a gentleman's residence.

Sixty-five acres of land, mainly pasture, went with the house in 1839, but much of this was detached from the "Rich, Park-like Grounds, embellished with a Fine Sheet of Water and magnificent Timber with Broad Terrace [on the east of the house]". The "magnificent Timber" was probably the result of Sir John Fellowes's lavish expenditure on "trees"; and also attributable to him was "the Carriage drive [which] passes through a stately avenue of Elms and Limes [some of which are still standing]." The Fellowes grotto is rather quaintly referred to in 1839 as "as Building planned as a Hermitage embosomed in Evergreens." Another old feature of the grounds was the "Rustic Summer House and Bridge" at the north end of the lake; but of this only the bridge (in a very dilapidated state) remains, though late 19th century photographs show that the summer house was still in existence then.

The history of the house was mentioned in only the briefest terms by the auctioneers in 1839; they totally ignored Carleton and Fellowes, but stated that it had been "Formerly the residence of Lord Chancellor Hardwicke". Nevertheless the distant past could not be completely disregarded. Some of the land which went with Carshalton House was copyhold, and, as the customs of the medieval manor were still being enforced against the well-off, one of the deceased's best beasts was forfeit to the lord of the Carshalton manor as a 'heriot' — a sort of fee for registering the transfer of the land in question. Actually, in Reynolds's case, the executors settled to pay £30 instead of surrendering a horse.

The purchaser of the premises (for £10,250) was Edward Simeon. In the Census returns of 1841 he figures as "Edward Simion, aged 52, Independent" and his household consisted only of a wife, aged 38, and a number of servants. By a pure coincidence he had come from Carleton Hall, Suffolk. I have found nothing else to indicate his social status, except the mention in his will of a brother, George, who was a baronet. The only thing recorded as having happened during

Edward Simeon's tenure of Carshalton House is a change made outside its walls. The water-obstructed highways of the village were becoming increasingly unacceptable as the 19th century advanced, and embanked roads through the town ponds had been built in the 1820s. Their construction was paid for by private subscriptions, and, apparently, it was not until 1846 that a sufficient number of public-spirited citizens were willing to finance a similar project for West Street. The Vestry met that year "to consider an improvement proposed to be made in the road leading through the water from the Cage *[the old lock-up at the bottom of Pound Street]* to West Street by raising the same. Mr. Simeon having proposed to make a by-road from the back of the Station House *[the Police Station had just been built on the north-east corner of Pound Street and the present West Street]* at the expense of certain subscriptions, it is proposed that the offer be accepted." Simeon headed the list of contributors with £50; and a new highway, then called Waterhouse Road but now regarded simply as the first part of West Street, came into existence. It was formed by raising the old ford through the water to the level of the foot-causeway. The pond which remained was later christened by John Ruskin 'Margaret's Well'; and the outfall of the Carshalton House lake was culverted under the new road to flow on by the side of the 'Old Rectory' and fall into the Upper Town Pond.

Brightling says that "Simeon removed in 1847 and let the premises for 21 years to the Board of Ordnance who had a preparatory school for the education of cadets for the Royal Artillery and Engineers". Simeon's reason for leaving Carshalton may have been a financial one, for the present title deeds of the house show that, in April 1849, he mortgaged the property for £8,405 (at 4%, the then current rate of interest!). He moved to Westhorpe House, Buckinghamshire, and was there when his will was made, on the 9th June 1851. He died that same year and he may have been incapacitated for some years previously, because, according to notes left by Arthur S. White concerning the history of the Ordnance School, it was actually Mrs. Simeon who leased Carshalton House — on the 2nd December 1848 at a rent of £360 per annum.

Earlier in his book, Brightling had remarked: "It is said that these premises were never let before the Board of Ordnance took their lease from Mr. Simeon, but had always been occupied by the owner." And, apart from the doubtful case of Lord Anson, that seems to have been a fact. But the change in occupancy which took place in 1848 was not just a matter of the difference between a freeholder and a lessee. It affected the status of the house itself. Thenceforth, except for two brief interludes, it ceased to be a private residence; and that circumstance was to result in great alterations being made in its ancillary buildings.

The Waterhouse was the first to be affected. On the 19th October 1848 the Bishop of the diocese granted "licence and authority for the performance of Divine Service in the Ordnance School at Carshalton House, which the Master General and Board of Ordnance intended to fit up and appropriate as and for the use of the Boys of the Establishment, such service to be performed by the Reverend Samuel Andrew, Clerk, the Headmaster of that School". It was in the Waterhouse that the new school's chapel was established, but there is some uncertainty as to exactly what part of it was appropriated to that purpose. Brightling seems not to have been aware of the Ordnance School's chapel in the Waterhouse, for he wrote: "the ground floor was an orangery and in 1867 it was converted

The Ordnance School and cadets. The Colonnade on the west of the mansion was then still open and without any structure above it. The cupola of the old stables appears on the left of the picture. On the extreme right is a corner of the 'Hermitage'.

83

into a neat Chapel." But if, as appears from Dr. Peatling's notes, orange trees were still growing in the orangery as late as 1872, it is more likely that the garden room facing the lake was the part of the Waterhouse used for religious worship. And the windows which now fill the tall arched openings may well date from this period.

The 80 cadets who were to assemble in the chapel were aged between 11 and 12 on admission to the school. They required nomination for the privilege, but the institution was expected to be self-supporting, so fees were charged — on a scale which took account of social and financial position. "Sons of Noblemen and Private Gentlemen, not being Officers in the Army or Navy" paid £110 per annum; £40 to £80 per annum was required, according to rank, for the sons of Officers; and "Sons of Officers of the Army and Navy who have died in the Service and whose Families are proved to be left in pecuniary distress" paid only £20 per annum. The course of instruction lasted 3 years or until the age of 15 was reached. An examination had then to be passed for entry into the Royal Military Academy, the prescribed subjects being English, Arithmetic, Algebra, Geometry, the Classics, French, German, Geography, History, Drawing and Printing (in manuscript). The required pass standards did not, however, make very formidable demands on the student.

The clothing each boy was to bring to the school was specified in the minutest detail, and no boy was to receive more than 1s. a week for pocket money (except for Monitors — what we should call Prefects — who could have 1s. 6d.). To stop any avoidence of this rule £1 was the maximum which any boy might start the term with. All these regulations — as is common with military establishments — read as if everything in the school was managed with exemplary care and competence. In fact, it was a small part of a grossly inefficient and divided organisation whose deficiencies led to the disasters of the Crimean War; and when, after the damage had been done, the administration of the British Army was radically reformed, the functions of the Board of Ordnance were taken over by the Secretary of State for War. *Jackson's Woolwich Journal* said in July 1855 that "the Ordnance School, having proved a complete failure, as was at the time predicted it would, is now to be abolished." But it was not finally closed until 1859.

Judging from the reminiscences of Sir Desmond O'Callaghan this came as a merciful release to the pupils. In a book called *Guns, gunners and others,* published in 1925, he gave an account of what was a distinguished Army career, beginning with a cadetship in the Carshalton establishment. Bluntly and briefly he condemned the Ordnance Board's place of instruction as a "thoroughly bad school". Some snobbishness may have lain behind this criticism, for he complained that "With the exception of three clergymen, not one of the masters had any resemblance to a gentleman, nor for the matter of that any pretensions in that direction." But the real cause for complaint was the reign of brutality in the school. Although official caning, "a terrible ordeal, before the whole school, was only inflicted for serious offences, and I am bound to say was of rare occurrence", the masters "ruled by force, and instruction was instilled by hard knuckles or the end of a ruler".

Fighting was officially recognised, and if two boys were found "hammering" each other unofficially, they were made, by the accepted code of conduct, to proceed "under rudimentary Queensbury rules" after school in "a large paved barn where there had already been provided a basin, towel and sponge." A master

Right to Left: The mansion; the Colonnade and conservatory over it; the dormitory built by Dr. Barrett.

Left to Right beside the drive: the old stables; (set back at the far end) the dining hall built by Dr. Barrett; (facing) the dormitory built by him.

85

apportioned the length of the rounds and schoolboy spectators cheered on the combatants. "There was no clinching in those days, so the weary cry 'Break away' was never heard. 'Hooks' were discouraged and straight hitting, well above the belt, was the order of the day. When both boys had had enough they very gladly shook hands and received, if they deserved it, the congratulations of both masters . . . and the other boys." On one occasion when the school was assembling for evening parade, the third class threw stones at the fourth class, following which there was "a general melee after evening school, in which blows were freely exchanged". The sequel was that next afternoon "before the whole school and in the presence of all the masters, the two classes of twenty little boys were drawn up in line and advanced towards each other", every boy selecting his adversary.

The author of *Guns, gunners and others* himself regarded all this officially approved fighting as "the only redeeming feature" of the establishment, since it resulted in "far less unofficial fighting than at any other school in England" (and, after all, the pupils were being trained to be a warrior class). What upset Sir Desmond originated in a raising of the age of admission to the Royal Military Academy from 14 to 16, which meant that boys had to stay on at Carshalton until they reached the latter age. "Bullying which, with boys of fourteen and under, was comparatively mild and harmless, now became very bad. A clique of the elders emulated each other in skilful and constructive cruelty . . . I saw a brute heat the tongs red hot in the fire of the sick room . . . dip them for a fraction of a second into some water in the sink and then seize another boy with them by the nose. The wound was a very bad one, and so long as I knew the boy the scar remained . . . the affair was apparently hushed up, and the brute eventually got his commission". Sir Desmond goes on to confess, almost with embarrassment, that when, as a Major, he much later on met this officer, then a Colonel, he refused to speak to him.

Another similar incident concerned "a poor chap who, like many school boys suffered from boils"; he was "so badly and so *accurately* beaten with a heavy stick that he had to go to hospital and was subsequently removed by his parents. He got his commission afterwards and was known as a brilliant mathematician." Sir Desmond himself was made "on a winter's night . . . to get out of bed and sit on a cold hearthstone over which water had been poured, and to remain there until the monitor or head of the room was asleep". On another winter's evening, hidden in a big yew tree, he had "listened to the stifled cries of a poor little chap strung up by the wrists and ankles to one of the lower horizontal branches for the edification of half a dozen young fiends, to whom the Chief Executioner explained that this was a Chinese torture at that time favoured by the celebrated 'Commissioner Yeh', but the points of suspension should be the thumbs and big toes; he didn't like to try that, as the boy would be so lame that the thing would be found out." (The sadistic Yeh Ming-chen, Viceroy of Canton, figured prominently in the Second Opium War (1856-1860), so this incident would date to the last years of the school's existence.)

Rather surprisingly, "no organised football was played, nor were any games patronised or helped in any way by the masters". But hockey and cricket were indulged in for the sake of "ingenious bullying. At hockey we were 'hacked' whether we were near the ball or not, and at cricket we were called up and beaten with a stump if, when fielding . . . we let a ball pass." I suppose it might be said that a British Army which could endure this sort of education could endure anything — as, indeed, it showed that it could at intervals during the 19th century. (Incidentally, by one of life's little ironies, Major General Desmond O'Callaghan was President of a reconstituted Ordnance Board from 1905 to 1908.)

According to Brightling — and he was now speaking of events which had occurred when he was adult — the remainder of the Ordnance Board's lease was "taken by Edmund Batt Esq., and the house occupied by him as a school for young gentlemen till 1862. It was then occupied for 12 months by Albert Pelly Esq." When the 1861 Census was taken on the 13th April, Edmund C. Batt, aged 45, a Member of the Royal College of Preceptors, was living in Carshalton House with his wife and two sons. There were only two pupils (aged 15 and 17) resident, but this was probably because Census Day fell within the Easter holidays. Staff still living on the premises included a Tutor aged 27 who was a "Professor of Music and Languages", a manservant, a cook, three housemaids, a kitchenmaid and a washerwoman. Why the school was given up so soon is not known.

Albert Pelly seems not to have intended a short stay in Carshalton House, because, when extensive alterations were made to the parish church in 1863, he went to the expense of having a new 'Faculty Seat' constructed. (Carshalton House — with three Faculty pews — had shared the gallery of the church with Carshalton Park since the time of Sir John Fellowes and Sir William Scawen.) The present title deeds of Carshalton House show that Pelly paid an architect three guineas for a plan and specification (dated March 1863) of the new Faculty Seat. But nothing now remains of it because the gallery and all the old seating disappeared when the church was practically rebuilt at the end of the 19th century. Albert Pelly made no lasting mark on Carshalton House either. But a son of his did. Among a number of names and initials scratched on the walls in various out of the way parts of the building Sister Pauline Stevens discovered the inscription "W. H. Pelly 1863".

It was in that year that the premises became once more a school. Edward Simeon's mortgagees and his widow, Eliza, joined in conveying Carshalton House on the 27th October 1863 to the "Reverend Alfred Barrett of North Cheam". The total price paid was £12,000, which was raised by a mortgage of £6,500 and the transfer of Consols (presumably Mr. Barrett's savings) to the vendors. According to an obituary notice in the *Sutton Herald* in 1887, the Reverend Alfred Barrett, D.D. "had for a long time conducted a school at North Cheam". (But his first two sons had been born in Highgate, the second as late as 1856.) When the 1861 Census was taken the North Cheam establishment had less than a dozen resident pupils, but, again, the rest were probably on holiday. A housekeeper, a wardrobe keeper, a nurse, four housemaids and a footman were 'living in' at the time, and they could not have been justified by such a small number of boarders. One of the latter was the son of a Colonel, another of a 'Reverend' and a third of a 'Registrar General' (but that may have described an official position in India because the boy was born in Madras).

The Reverend Alfred Barrett (he was then "M.A. Oxon" and evidently obtained his Doctorate in Divinity subsequently) was described in the Census return as "Chaplain of Temporary Church, Sutton, Surrey"; and the obituary notice said that he "had a Church in the Cheam Road, Sutton . . . at which he ministered on Sundays. This Church was used whilst the present Sutton Parish Church was being rebuilt, and was shortly afterwards pulled down." By an odd coincidence 1863 was the year in which, because Carshalton church was being extensively altered, the Waterhouse chapel was licensed "for the performance of the several offices of Divine Service" for the benefit of all parishioners. When All Saints' church was re-opened, the new owner of Carshalton House took advantage of this licence to continue holding public services in the Waterhouse chapel. And, according to the obituarist already quoted, this was "a circumstance which, we have heard, caused some unpleasantness between Mr. Cator, the late rector, and Dr. Barrett, the former appealing to the Bishop to interfere". The result of the appeal is not stated. It is likely that Mr. Cator, a most conservative churchman, had been upset because his fellow clergyman was expressing, in his sermons, views which were not entirely orthodox. Certainly, the self-appointed incumbent of the Waterhouse chapel seems to have felt a very strong personal call to preach the gospel even when official exponents of it were available.

It is a pity that we do not know more about Dr. Barrett, for he was undoubtedly a 'character'. All that the obituary vouchsafed on this was that he "owed his fortunes in life mainly to his own industry, a fact of which he was in no way ashamed, but of which, on the contrary, he was rather proud." Beyond that, all that I have been able to discover about his private life is that he was born in Brackley, Northants in 1816, married a widow in 1850 and had three sons. Outside religious matters he apparently made no attempt to play a public role; his obituarist said that he "always lived a retired life, taking no part in the politics of the village". Nevertheless "his kindliness of disposition and charitableness made him much esteemed amongst his neighbours, both rich and poor alike". And another newspaper report shows him, only a few weeks before his death, making his premises available for Carshalton's celebrations of Queen Victoria's Golden Jubilee.

As a schoolmaster Dr. Barrett obviously satisfied contemporary requirements; his move from North Cheam to much larger premises is proof of his success in his secular profession. When the 1871 Census was taken there were living in Carshalton House, besides boy pupils, four young girls aged from 4 to 9 and a "Governess" aged 22, whose presence undoubtedly betokened the girls' school which Mrs. Barrett was running at that time. The boys had one "Tutor" aged 33 and another aged 18. But the domestic staff required for the establishment far outnumbered the academics; it comprised a Housekeeper, two Matrons, a Nurse, a Needlewoman, three House Maids, two Kitchen Maids, three Laundry Maids, a Footman and a Houseboy. Forty-four boys aged between 5 and 19 were listed; eight were born in the East Indies, two in India and one in Australia (Dr. Barrett's enterprise depended very heavily on its appeal to expatriate parents). Although Census Day was the 10th April, it seems, judging from the number of resident pupils and staff, that this was not within the school holiday. If it had been, the Census taker would have been unlikely to have found in Josiah Baines's 'Leicester House' school on the Wrythe two assistant masters aged 24 and 17, two pupil teachers aged 14, five servants and forty-nine boys.

The Carshalton House establishment was undoubtedly a much more 'classy' one; and, in the end, it probably also exceeded 'Leicester House' in numbers. At any rate, the obituary in the *Sutton Herald* said that "when the school at Carshalton was in its prime there was frequently over one hundred pupils there, and the

The 'Hermitage' and boathouse in Dr. Barrett's time.

The 'Hermitage in 1976 from the now dried-up lake.

Carshalton House Cricket and Football Clubs were well known in local circles."

Whatever the size of the school, it undoubtedly constituted a very profitable business to begin with. Brightling, writing in 1872, was able to report: "It has lately been much improved by the addition of a large dining-room, dormitories and other buildings", which must have involved a considerable capital expenditure. It seems that the boys of the Ordnance School had been accommodated for eating – and perhaps, to some extent, for sleeping – in the house itself; and what Dr. Barrett had done was to replace the old Brewhouse, Washhouse and Dairy to the west of the mansion by something a sale catalogue of 1888 called a "Wing" (possibly incorporating some of the fabric of the old buildings) which contained, on the ground floor, seven servants' bedrooms and an infirmary, while above were the boys' dormitories. Probably to enable those latter to be supervised from the mansion a connecting "lofty span-roof conservatory" had been built over the Colonnade, but it is not clear whether that 'entrée' had, at this time, been enclosed.

The dining room spoken of by Brightling acted also as the school assembly hall; it continued northwards the line of the stable block, and measured 64' by 27'6", with a gallery at one end and a vestibule at the other. Communicating with it were a Pantry, a "Washing Room fitted with lavatories" and a "Matron's Room with large presses", the whole area being heated by hot water pipes in the latest fashion. (Dr. Barrett's dining room, washing room and matron's room still exist in the modern school buildings, though they now serve other purposes.)

The school-rooms used by Dr. Barrett – also heated by hot water pipes – may have been among the "other buildings" which Brightling says he added; or they may have been adaptations which dated from the Ordnance Board's time. Whoever was responsible, the sale catalogue of 1888 makes it clear that somebody had converted the accommodation originally provided for horses and carriages into rooms where a very different kind of grooming and coaching could be given. What was described as "Formerly the Stabling Department" had become "four large and lofty School Rooms, a small Study and Room adjoining, another large School Room and 6 rooms at the end of the block", while, in "the Spacious Enclosed Yard" at the rear was a "large timber and tiled Barn with asphalte [sic] floor which has been used as a Drill and Play Room". That latter was almost certainly an Ordnance School conversion; Sir Desmond O'Callaghan spoke of a large barn used as a drill hall. (In actual fact, though, the 'barn' was probably the old coach house.)

In 1883 Dr. Barrett brought County Court proceedings against General Julian Hobson for a term's fees in lieu of notice, following the withdrawal from the school of Julian Hobson junior. Counsel's brief together with documentary evidence to be used in the case have been deposited in the Surrey Record Office, and, from these papers, some interesting information about Carshalton House school can be obtained. Dr. Barrett is stated to have been "for the past 33 years engaged in keeping a School, commencing at Highgate, then at North Cheam, and afterwards at Carshalton House". He begins a printed prospectus for this last school with the following potted (and inaccurate) history of the premises: "The Site of this Mansion was originally chosen by the celebrated Dr. Radcliffe. It is said that some of the Books placed in his noble Library at Oxford were collected at Carshalton. The House was afterwards very much enlarged and improved by Sir

John Fellowes and Lord Chancellor Hardwicke. It eventually became the seat of the late Mr. Simeon. Some years ago Her Majesty's Government took a Lease of the Premises and fitted them up, regardless of expense, as the Royal Ordnance School. The Dormitories, Baths, School Rooms etc. are excellent. Many of the officers of the Royal Artillery and Engineers must retain a vivid recollection of the merits of the House and Grounds. *[But not Sir Desmond O'Callaghan.]* A large Hall and extensive Dormitories have since been added by the present Head Master."

The prospectus continued: "Dr. Barrett has spared no exertions to place the School in a proper position. His pupils have gained very high honours in competing for the Indian Civil Service, for the Royal Artillery, for admission into Sandhurst etc. Several have become King's Scholars and Prizemen at Eton. Others have obtained an excellent position at Rugby, and also in Oxford and Cambridge examinations. The Engineering pupils have been equally successful. Sound preparatory Teaching is given, as well as advanced Instruction. Modern Languages, Geometrical, Mechanical and Landscape Drawing are carefully taught."

Notes of examination successes achieved by pupils suggest that Dr. Barrett specialised in getting boys through the Army entrance examination. And what he could offer at Carshalton House appealed particularly to officers serving in India who needed, above all, a school which would also serve as a home in England for their children. Here Mrs. Barrett's girls' school was very useful, because it meant that whole families could be accommodated; and a reduction was offered for taking a quantity. The printed prospectus proclaimed the school fees to be 100 guineas per annum (which covered clothing but not medical expenses); Major (as he then was) Hobson, however, got his two boys accepted at 60 guineas each and his two girls at 50 guineas each. Unfortunately, in 1876, the state of Mrs. Barrett's health forced her to give up the girls' school, and the younger Hobson boy left with his two sisters. Their father realised that he would have to pay more for Julian alone and offered £75 a year, which Dr. Barrett agreed to without demur.

Letters from both Hobson parents over a number of years indicate a very cordial relationship with the Barretts and contain frequent expressions of gratitude for the way in which the children were being looked after. But the General's son and heir was not by any means a model pupil. In 1876 his father was urging that the boy be put to learning Greek, but this was an over-ambitious project. In the court proceedings Julie (as his parents, rather oddly to our ears, called him) was described as "of average ability but very lazy, and there was great difficulty in getting him to work . . . . On the occasion of *[his]* going up for the *[Army entrance]* examination the first time he left before the examination was over." Nevertheless he did pass at a second attempt, and stayed for another term until Christmas 1881. Then, in the holidays, his father (back in England by now) got a tutor for him and was so satisfied with the results that he decided to remove the boy from the school and have him "working under my eye". But when Dr. Barrett politely asked for £25, a term's fees in lieu of notice, General Hobson objected very strongly and threatened, if the case were brought to court, to "expose the school", complaining that his son's education had been neglected. The County Court judge did, in fact, decide against Dr. Barrett, but this seems to have been, not because of a failure to give value for money, but owing to the absence of a specific requirement for a term's notice in the arrangements agreed with General

Hobson. A claim for £6. 11s. "extras" had had to be abandoned because proving it would have involved calling Mrs. Barrett as a witness (she kept the school's accounts) and the ordeal, it was feared, would have overtaxed her strength.

The paper ammunition supplied to Dr. Barrett's counsel included young Julian's "Offence Sheet". Nowadays juvenile delinquency is no laughing matter, but Master Hobson's crimes make almost hilarious reading, and were probably not regarded as very serious at the time — though it was an age which certainly believed in the social value of teaching the young to obey rules. Julie's worst misdemeanour, for which he was flogged, was being "Out of Bounds (in High St.) about 3 p.m. on Derby Day". When "Reported by the Butler for purloining Bread" he had to go without his supper. But the usual school punishments of learning verses of poetry, or the conjugations of French verbs, or passages from a history book were imposed for the offences of "Playing Clappers in Bedroom", "Out of Bed and not undressed at 8.45 p.m.", "Noise & Wrestling opposite Doctor's Study door after prayers", "Impertinence to Mr. Cambridge", and "Disrespect to Matron". However, against "Bolster fighting at ¼ to 9 p.m." there is a note "Denies", and no punishment is recorded. Young Hobson was frequently late for "Hall Parade" and "Drill", once "Whereby keeping the Rev. Barrett waiting". Perhaps he found it difficult to get up in the morning because he was over-active at night. On one occasion he was "not in his Bedroom at 9.15 p.m. He Skunked up some time afterwards with Boots on". And, another time, he was seen to "secrete a light of some description in his Bed at 9 p.m. on Saturday night." At about this time he was in urgent financial need and wrote to an uncle asking for a Postal Order for 7s. 6d. to spend on a forthcoming half-holiday when Dr. Barrett would allow his pupils to go into the village and buy what they liked. But Julie had made a bad misjudgment in his man. The uncle had only recently returned from India having had nothing to do with his nephew for years, and he sent the begging letter to Dr. Barrett with a request that steps be taken "to stop the ungentlemanly habit the boy seems to have fallen into". The only recorded 'punishment', however, is a copy of an abject letter of apology from the delinquent to his uncle.

He does not seem to have been uniquely naughty in the School. There are frequent instances recorded of lateness for Roll Call and for Dinner or Tea; one report reads: "At Roll Call I have not ten on Parade. Nearly all were present for Hall, but most of them with their hair not dressed and their slippers on." Pupils en masse could be guilty of disorderly conduct, too. On one occasion "The Choir party misbehaved very much going to Afternoon chapel. They ran away from the Doctor and were talking and laughing in a loud tone. I [? *Charles Barrett*] had to leave my party and Halt them twice". And one boy actually "Fell in on Parade for afternoon Chapel with a School cap on."

Dr. Barrett's obituarist said that "with advancing age the learned doctor was unable to give the school the attention it had formerly received, and, as his son did not care to follow the scholastic profession, it gradually dwindled down until it was given up altogether." This seems to have been an attempt to spare the feelings of the living, but it was unfair to the deceased. Dr. Barrett is unlikely to have made the capital investment represented by his additions to the premises without having had good reason to believe that his eldest son, Charles, would carry on the business. And, in fact, the latter did "follow the scholastic profession" for some years as an assistant to his father. (It was he who had "the chief care and tuition" of young Julian Hobson, so he must have taken the senior boys.) In January 1882 a formal partnership deed (the draft is in the Surrey Record Office) was drawn up between father and son, and, in the Court case the following year, Charles was described as his father's partner. By now the "learned doctor" was 67 years old and could reasonably have expected much of the burden of the school's management to be taken off his shoulders by his son. In the circumstances, Charles can hardly be held blameless for the "dwindling down" of the business — though he may well have been temperamentally unsuited to follow the career his father had chosen. An additional mortgage of £2,000 raised in 1881 suggests that the Barrett finances were already in decline then. And a printed prospectus of the partnership in the papers appertaining to the Court case shows a sad deterioration in the pretensions of the school. Fees were quoted thus: "Daily Pupils 6 gns. a term. Daily Boarders 12 gns. a term. Weekly Boarders 17 gns. a term. Stationery, Dancing & Drilling will be moderate Extras". But it was explicitly stated: "A term's notice required before removal."

Dr. Barrett's will, made in 1885, left Carshalton House to his eldest son, Charles, with a direction that he should maintain his mother. But she was not to require a school or any part of the estate to be sold to the detriment of either property "should my said son Charles carry on a school either at Carshalton House aforesaid or elsewhere." The only income the widow could expect in her own right was to come from investing the proceeds of a sale of certain of her husband's books together with his collection of minerals and geological specimens.

Concerning Dr. Barrett's death in 1887, his obituarist wrote that he "had been in ill health for some time, death being due to natural decay, the deceased being 71 years of age." Medical science has progressed since his time and natural decay at the age of 71 would not nowadays be an accepted cause of death.

What Charles Raymond Booth Barrett did for a living — if anything — after the closure of the school, I have not discovered. He was born at Highgate in 1850, took an M.A. degree at Pembroke College, Oxford, and married the daughter of a Major General in the Indian Army. (His two younger brothers both reached high rank in that Army.) He was an enthusiastic researcher into the past, publishing a number of articles on subjects of antiquarian interest, and also the book already mentioned, called *Surrey: Highways, Byways and Waterways*. But his literary work could not have been financially very rewarding, and certainly would not have supported a Carshalton House style of living. A large part of what he wrote was never printed, and much of it was passed by his widow to Dr. Peatling. Among these literary remains are indications that, at one time, Charles Barrett contemplated writing a history of Carshalton. But he never even completed the first chapter, because he could not resist digressions to display his enormous erudition about the early Norman period in English history. To us his most valuable contribution to the study of the past is what he wrote about Carshalton House. Unfortunately, though, he did not always give the sources of his information; and as he showed himself to be a man of very strong prejudices and dislikes (Brightling — whom he described as an "illiterate man" — was one of his pet aversions), not all his statements can be unquestioningly accepted as accurate.

It is pretty certain that, soon after his father's death, Charles Barrett began to find the upkeep of Carshalton House beyond his means. Sister Pauline Stevens's researches have established that, in 1888, he moved to an address in Wandsworth; and the sale catalogue of 1888, to which reference has been made, contains the highly significant note: "The vendor is a mortgagee selling under his statutory power of sale, and the concurrence of the owners of the equity of redemption [*i.e. the freeholder*] shall not be required." (Sister Pauline Stevens discovered a copy of this catalogue, not in the Kingston Record Office, but in the Guildford one.) The auctioneers advertised the premises as "eminently adapted for a Hydropathic or Scholastic Establishment, or for a Public Institution" and added that "parts could be advantageously utilized for Building purposes, leaving the Mansion and the chief part of the Pleasure Grounds intact." But all these attractions evidently failed to produce a bid which would pay off the mortgage, for Carshalton House remained in the property market. In 1890 its rateable value was reduced from £255 to £85, probably because a large part of the premises was not now being used at all. Then Carshalton Urban District Council, looking for a site for a Recreation Ground, offered to buy some six acres of the land which went with Carshalton House, but the property was only for sale as a whole. Finally, in October 1893, a buyer was found in the Daughters of the Cross, who saw in the premises room for an additional Convent, an English Novitiate and the schools they wished to establish. The first boarders actually arrived on the 31st October, and the following year, the rateable value, not surprisingly, went up to £340.

The Daughters of the Cross were — and are — a Roman Catholic order founded in Liège in 1833, but with 'Provinces' in a number of countries. The buildings they had now acquired in England, having been empty for five years, were, naturally, in poor condition; but the Sisters set to work vigorously to repair the ravages of time and neglect, and very soon they were starting to put up new buildings. It is evident, from the 1888 sale catalogue, that some of the amenities that had come with their purchase dated back to the Carleton/Fellowes era. There were still "a fine old octagonal Dovecote", "a large Drying and Poultry Yard", and a farmyard with "a 2-Stall Stable, Coach House and Loft, Poultry Houses, Slaughter House, Cow Shed, Piggeries, Wood Shed and Mushroom Houses with Granary over" (but the mushrooms were probably a 19th century introduction). The catalogue also mentions "a stone-built GROTTO SUMMER HOUSE called 'The Hermitage' "; an Ice House; an Orchard; 3 Large Walled Kitchen Gardens with Greenhouse, 2 Vineries, Potting Sheds and Apple Room; also a Laundry with 2 large boilers and supplies of hot, cold and soft water; Ironing Room; Boiler House; and a Range of Poultry House, Coal House and Outside W.C. A prominent feature of the landscape was still the "Large Ornamental Lake (with Island) supplied by never-failing Springs, which yield an abundance of water of excellent quality capable of being turned to very profitable account." (Perhaps because the lake was "well stocked with Trout".) And, finally, there was the "Red Brick Building comprising Chapel, Pump House (with pumping apparatus worked by an undershot wheel, with supply pipes to the Mansion and throughout the Premises); also a LARGE PLUNGE BATH, the walls lined with Dutch tiles, with Dressing Room adjoining", together with "large Cisterns on the Water Tower."

The mansion itself was very much as it had been in 1839. On the top floor, in addition to a Housemaid's Room, a W.C. and a Bath Room, there were still seven bedrooms and four dressing rooms; the main bedrooms on the first floor still possessed their 18th century mantelpieces and marble window seats, a

Bird's-eye view c.1902. All the buildings shown in the views on page 85 are depicted. The convent church is a new construction. The top of the dovecote can be seen just to the right of the cupola of Dr. Barrett's dormitory building.

95

number also having an "alcoved recess" for the bed. Six reception rooms still occupied most of the ground floor; but the Painted Parlour was now called a "Second Library or Smoking Room" and had been "fitted with book shelves with cupboards under". (The damage done by these attachments, later removed, is still visible, and it is to be hoped, for the sake of the reputation of the Barretts, that they were not responsible for this piece of vandalism.) The domestic offices were still in the basement, and now included "a Bake House with bread oven . . . communicating with Bread Room", and "a Dairy & Salting Room".

The dairy must have continued to be useful to the Daughters of the Cross for a time, because I can remember, as a boy, seeing mysterious habited figures leading a small herd of cows through a door in the wall flanking what we called the 'cinderpath' into the meadow which lay between that public footway and the railway line. The meadow was actually a small part of the area called 'Coulsons or Coulsdens' or 'Colstons', which had for long gone with Carshalton House and originally stretched nearly to the Wrythe. The coming of the railway had divided it, and the lower part was first incorporated in Short's Farm and later built on after Colston Avenue had been cut through it.

That last 'development' of Carshalton occurred soon after the First World War and, by that time, the grounds of Carshalton House had also been developed. The needs of both the Convent and a rapidly expanding educational field had obliged the Daughters of the Cross to embark on a building programme which not only covered some previously open ground but also replaced old constructions with new ones. A religious order cannot be criticised for devoting to the purposes for which it exists money that otherwise would have to be spent on maintaining and repairing secular buildings which have outlived their usefulness. But, in purely material terms, the ultimate result of the devoted work of the Sisters has been that, although a great deal of the 18th century could still be seen on the site at the end of the 19th century, now all that Sir John Fellowes would recognise is the mansion, the Waterhouse, the Hermitage, the boundary wall and the piers of the entrance gates. Against that, it should be said that, if the estate had not belonged to a religious body for which commercial considerations were of secondary importance, the land would, almost certainly, have been sold for housing 'developments' and Carshalton House, together with its Waterhouse, would long since have been demolished, as all the other 18th century mansions in Carshalton have been.

CHAPTER NINE

St. Philomena's

I hope that nobody will think it male presumption on my part to offer an account of a girls' school; I should not have ventured — or been able — to tackle the subject if the present Superior of the Convent, Sister Mary Gemma, had not very kindly loaned me some old copies of the school magazine, 'The Philomena', and if Sister Pauline Stevens had not supplemented the information I obtained from those with her own knowledge of the history of the school.

A 1915 issue of the magazine gives a charming story of how Carshalton House, after its purchase by the Daughters of the Cross, became 'St. Philomena's' (though the Convent itself is actually dedicated to 'Our Lady of Dolours'). "Once upon a time", the tale begins, "the good priest of Sutton was in great distress. The old iron building that had served him as a school had been condemned." The only chance the children now had of getting a Catholic education was, it seemed to him, to be taught by Religious. But there was no convent anywhere near. In his difficulty the priest appropriately turned to a child saint and "sent money for Masses to be said in his intention at the altar of St. Philomena in Ars." At the very same time the Provincial Superior of the Daughters of the Cross was looking for a suitable English house, and she prayed to St. Philomena to find her one. Both prayers were answered when Carshalton House was discovered to be in the market. As soon as the Convent was established "Sisters used to go to Sutton every day to teach the children in the sacristy of the Church."

A more prosaic account of the origin of the school's name, given in a 1973 issue of the magazine (kindly lent to me by Mrs. Kathleen Beckey), says that St. Philomena was chosen as the establishment's patroness on the advice of Father Charles Bowden, who was very learned in Roman archaeology and believed that a gravestone discovered in the catacomb of St. Priscilla was that of Filumena (*Child of Light*). Whatever the truth of the matter may be, it is certain that one of the first new buildings to be commissioned by the Daughters of the Cross — in 1896 — was what was then called an 'elementary' school, which they named 'St. Mary's'. It fronted Short's Road and was well clear of existing buildings in the grounds, so no demolition preceded its construction.

Elementary schools, in those days, provided state-supported, free education for children aged from 5 to 14. In the 1890s there were so few Catholic families in the district that, to begin with, according to the 1915 article in *The*

Philomena, "nine out of every ten of the children *[in St. Mary's]* were Protestants". "But", the account continues, "the proportion of Catholic children steadily increased *[and the school had to be enlarged]* and now out of a total of over 200, at least 140 are Catholics. The school is for boys and girls, and excellent work is done there. Several scholarships for secondary schools have been gained from time to time." The pupils of St. Mary's had responded patriotically, too, to the demands made by the First World War. During its first winter "they collected among themselves 11s. 6d. to send to Princess Mary's Fund and very proud they are of the letter of thanks from Buckingham Palace. In addition they have sent five blankets and three dozen handkerchiefs for the soldiers at the front, and the girls are busy knitting so as to have more things to send." Twenty old boys of the school had, by then, enlisted in the armed forces, two were already dead, two more were prisoners of war, and several had been wounded.

St. Mary's was, however, only a part of the educational complex which the teaching activities of the Daughters of the Cross eventually created at Carshalton House. Their principal and first established school was St. Philomena's College, described in advertisements as a "High-class Boarding School". In 1893 some twenty pupils had been in St. Wilfrid's Convent, Chelsea, ready for transfer to Carshalton House as soon as it was acquired. Their number quickly grew to forty, and, in the end, it reached a high point of about a hundred and twenty; but, after the First World War, the intake began to fall off – principally, I suspect, because there were by then a good many excellent day secondary schools for girls. The fees charged, 60 guineas per annum, were certainly not prohibitive.

St. Philomena's had very quickly won a high reputation both in this country and abroad, attracting pupils from, literally, all over the world. Some of them, like those in Dr. Barrett's school, had English parents who were working and living overseas. But, just as young ladies from England used once to go over the Channel to be 'finished', so, too, there was a 'Finishing Class' at St. Philomena's for foreign girls. Sister Pauline Stevens came across the following account, rendered in 1904 to the parents of one of them, which reveals big changes in the value of money since those pre-Great War days.

Pension for 29 weeks (Dec. 23rd to July 30th)	£29. 0s. 0d.
Stationery and stamps	18s. 9d.
Use of books (8s.) and subscriptions to Clubs	18s. 6d.
Shoemaker's account	2s. 0d.
Medicine and medical attendance	2s. 0d.
Clothing	£ 5. 17s. 4d.
Silk blouse (14s. 6d.); Hats (9s. 6d.)	£ 1. 4s. 0d.
Dancing lessons (1½ terms)	£ 1. 11s. 6d.

Pupils from Germany were so numerous that they even formed in that country an Old Philomenians Club (which, not surprisingly, did not meet during the First World War, but was revived soon afterwards). Some girls came to the school with little knowledge of English, and, in an early issue of *The Philomena* there is a good-natured story about a pupil who expressed an earnest desire to learn sense, but made it clear that she expected to do so in a laboratory. Command of the language was soon acquired in such an environment, and the review of a concert given by girls who remained in the school during the 1913 Christmas holidays specially mentioned one singer whose "every word was understood in spite of the

The boys' prep. school c. 1912.

Boating on the lake by pupils of St. Philomena's c.1912.

fact that /she/ is a foreigner and has been with us for one term only."

In those pre-air-travel days, the girls from abroad, together with those whose parents lived and worked in distant lands, had to spend their holidays in the school. But, judging from what they wrote in the school magazine, they did not find the experience depressing. One account of Christmas in the school ended "I think we were agreed that we would like to begin all over again." The festivities had started on Christmas Eve with a Christmas tree and presents, after which came an early retirement to bed at 6 o'clock, then an awakening for Midnight Mass, more bed following buns and cocoa, and finally turkey on Christmas Day itself.

The pupils who spent their holidays in the school were at least spared the ordeal endured by returning girls on 'Re-opening Day' in January 1923 when they encountered that phenomenon known to old-time Londoners as a 'pea-souper'. The two Sisters who were to escort the girls on the train from London left Carshalton by the 3.3 train instead of the normal 5 o'clock one in order to be more certain of arriving at the terminus in time for the 6.10 back. As it turned out, they were in time for the 5.30., which did not leave Victoria until an hour later. But when it came into the platform, the seething mass of maddened commuters swept aside the Philomenians, paying no attention to the 'Reserved' notice on some of the carriages. One Sister and half the girls were left behind while "the lucky ones – if such they could be called – had to be content to travel twenty-four in one compartment". They reached Carshalton at 8 p.m.; and "the second party arrived at 9 p.m. having been taken to Sutton", from whence they presumably made their way to Carshalton House by tram – or Shanks's pony. Then, at 9.45, when everybody had gone to bed, "the Irish and Northern girls", who had been given up as lost for the time being, turned up "looking quite delighted with themselves". (Such experiences can, of course, be enjoyable when one is young.) The following day "Cars, taxis, cabs arrived every hour of the morning", and "by lunch time practically everyone had come." But there were no lessons that day, so the girls had some compensation for their tribulations. They would not nowadays be so much inconvenienced by fog, but might be in an even worse plight as a result of what is euphemistically called 'industrial action' but does not mean 'work'.

St. Philomena's was open to girls of all ages from about three upwards, and besides the usual school subjects, it undertook to teach "First Aid, Home Nursing, Cookery and Dressmaking". Naturally, religious instruction was an important feature of the education provided, but bodies were catered for as well as souls. There was boating on what one school writer called "the Lake of Shining Waters"; and, according to an article in a 1973 issue of *Philomena,* "a skiff, a punt, a canoe and small dinghies" were available to the pupils. But enjoyment of the lake was interrupted in 1907 when a particularly fierce swan, on whom the name of 'Dreyfus' was conferred, made it necessary for a fence to be constructed for the protection of humans. Generally, however, wild life on the water was a source of pleasure, and there are frequent references in the school magazine not only fo swans nesting, but to more modest – and less dangerous – entertainment provided by ducks, moorhens and dabchicks. However, it was not the custom of the time to treat all birds with respect, and in 1912 *The Philomena* reported that "The school museum has been enriched by a beautiful stuffed heron", which had been shot in the grounds and "was such a fine specimen as to be well worth preserving."

Top: The school orchestra, and below: the hockey team; both pictures date from c.1912.

In the 1920s the lake began to disappear in dry seasons, and, in the end, there was no water in it except after very heavy rainfall. That put an end to boating activities and also to its natural inhabitants. The latter may not have welcomed the intrusion of oars into their home, but, at least, they had never been disturbed by girls having swimming lessons. There was a heated bath, built in 1909, for that kind of sport. It stood — and still stands — near the Waterhouse, and originally had beside it the old Summer House by the 'Bridge'. (The semi-circular flight of stone steps at the entrance to the swimming bath is believed to be the one which once led up to the Colonnade.)

Somewhat earlier, about 1900, a Bicycle Path had been laid out so that pupils could, in safety, indulge in what was then a fashionable pastime. The Bicycle Path actually followed the line of a 'walk' through the old 'Wilderness', running southwestwards from the Waterhouse to the stable block at a short distance from the boundary wall. It cannot have been safe for anyone else to venture along this modernised antiquity which, in its modest way, was heralding the age of mechanised transport by road. But there were plenty of opportunities for other games. By 1910 three tennis courts had been laid out; and the girls also indulged in basket ball. But it was hockey which aroused their greatest enthusiasm; during the season, there were practice games every day and, by 1921, the playing fields covered an acre and a half. Even the foreign girls became addicted to hockey. In 1913 a German ex-pupil, back in her own country, wrote: "Are the girls still so eager about their Hockey? I have learned to love it more than I did even at Carshalton, because here it means getting out of the town into the country . . . . It takes quite an hour to get to the 'Sportplatz', but we don't mind that because we find ourselves there in the midst of the forest, miles away from the noise of the metropolis. We often have competition games, and for this purpose Hockey journeys have to be arranged. How merry these are! A short time ago (in January) we beat Stettin 6 - 0; it was a most difficult game, as the place was covered with snow and one kept on sliding and gliding." (Was this how ice hockey originated?)

A hockey match between Past and Present pupils was always a much-looked-forward-to feature of the celebrations which marked the most important event of the year in the school calendar — the 10th October, St. Philomena's Day. (The Old Girls seem not to have kept up their former standards of training, because they were usually beaten.) This great day invariably ended with a Fancy Dress Ball, the costumes for which were ingeniously devised and executed by the girls in coloured crepe paper. During the course of an evening's dancing this attire, not surprisingly, began to disintegrate, but, as there were no male partners, nobody worried unduly. The Fancy Dress Ball was preceded by a Concert given in annual turn by each form in the school, even the 'Babies' having their moment of glory. But the shape of things to come began to disclose itself in 1923 when there was "a surprise which we appreciated very much" in the form of a "Wireless Concert".

Other feast days were also marked by Concerts; but religious occasions were not just an excuse for jollification. Due emphasis was always placed on the serious side of life, and giving to others was practised on a community basis through Charity Bazaars. One of these, organised in 1913 — with an up-to-date entertainment from a gramophone as an additional attraction — brought in £28. 19s. 2d. ("£5 more than last year"); and, with this, to our inflated ideas, meagre sum,

Christmas hampers were made up for distribution to the poor of the district and special treats were also provided for their children. All this followed a very old tradition of alms-giving; in fact, at the beginning of this century, the social attitude of the well-off towards what are now called the 'under privileged' had not changed much since the 18th century. A writer in *The Philomena* reported, after the distribution in 1913, "each child came up in its turn and received either an article of clothing or a strong pair of boots, or, if it were in better circumstances, a toy; but all were equally delighted and satisfied with whatever was given them. One poor little boy who came to try on a pair of boots had only half a stocking, which he blushingly tried to pull over his foot; and then, as if to add to his dismay, the boots were found to be too small for him. Poor little fellow — he looked the picture of misery and dejection when he realized he was not to have any boots at all. We could not resist the feelings of generosity that came over us and asked Sister to send out into the village for a pair of stockings and good strong boots, while we decided we would each pay a small sum to complete the total expense. His face literally glowed with delight when the boots and stockings were finally fitted on his feet, and he strode out of the room with a proud air — looking at his feet the whole time. And a happy Christmas we did have . . . by the thought that we had brought a ray of sunshine into these poverty-stricken homes." It is easy to make fun of these sentiments or to wax morally indignant over past social evils; and it is undeniably a good thing that present-day children do not go unshod for want of money (though their feet may come to much worse harm through ill-fitting shoes if juvenile fashion so dictates). But the modern tax and rate payer who nowadays provides a blanket insurance against destitution does so with no charitable feelings, while the recipient of the largesse from the state which has replaced personal alms-giving is given no sense of human kindness. And, in those respects, we are spiritually the poorer.

During the 'Great War' 'good works' were, of course, concentrated on supplying comforts to the armed forces; and *The Philomena* reported that "knitting for the soldiers" had replaced "getting up songs and dramatic representations for a Concert". Fifty pounds was raised by a Bazaar in 1915 and this sum paid for flannel shirts, mufflers, helmets and bedsocks "to make life in the Trenches a little more bearable during the cold winter months."

Of course, no German girls came to St. Philomena's between 1914 and 1918, but the school continued to maintain its numbers at about 100, the figure which Dr. Barrett's school, too, had attained in its prime. *The Philomena* also went on chronicling, every two months, the activities of the school; and, even after the war, its subscription rate was kept at 3s. per annum (15p. in present-day money). The Editor was always one of the Sisters, but most of the contributions came from pupils, present and past; and the literary standard of the stories, poems and essays published was a credit to the teachers of the writers. To have a letter accepted was an honour eagerly sought and not easily won. One very young aspirant wrote: "I am trying very hard to get my letter printed, and, if it is, all at home will be pleased with me, and I am longing to see it in the Mag. This term I am going to get clever. I am going to try and get the Bishop's prize this year . . . . The night Father Christmas came I was so excited about the toys that I got up before it was time and emptied the pillow case. *[Its contents included "a sweet little doll, a little bird that could cry and two little rocking chairs".]* We also had a

Christmas tree with lovely toys on, but the candles were not lit because the leaves would burn, and a cake with a statue of Father Christmas on, holding in his hand some ivy, which looked very pretty indeed. I am trying to make my letter very interesting and better than before. I must now say good-bye, with love and kisses, I remain, Your affectionate little Philomenian." Could any editor have had the heart to reject that effusion?

Senior girls, of course, made more sophisticated contributions to the school magazine. One, published in a 1922 issue, has already been mentioned for its imaginative account – supposedly from the mouth of a patriarchal frog – of Dr. Radcliffe and his connection with Carshalton House. This old inhabitant of the lake, obviously misled by the currently accepted human authorities, went on to say that "the lovely mansion was entirely rebuilt" by Sir John Fellowes. Then comes the extraordinary statement: "the Black Rat reported to me the following written fragment which it had come across while exploring on Sir John's desk: Pay to Sir Christopher Wren for the designing of the mansion the sum of . . . . (The Black Rat could not remember the amount.)" Who, I wonder, was responsible for the idea that Carshalton House was designed by Wren? Even Sister Pauline Stevens could not supply an answer to that question; but she did point out that it has always been taken for granted that Carshalton House must have been the work of a top architect, and it has even been attributed to Inigo Jones (who died in 1652, when The Old Farm was still standing).

After the death of Sir John Fellowes the article has the next owner as Lord Chancellor Hardwicke, who, it says, "further beautified the mansion. Two famous designers, brothers . . . whose names were . . . Adam, richly decorated the alcoved dining-room with which Lord Hardwicke . . . was greatly pleased". (But, actually he had left Carshalton House long before the Adam brothers started working in England.) From Lord Hardwicke the Frog's memory jumped first to the "preparatory school for the Artillery and Engineer Cadets", of which he gave no details, and then to Dr. Barrett's school, the boys of which, he said, were very cruel to the wild life in the grounds. The article goes on to say that, in Dr. Barrett's time, "a wing was built containing dormitories and class-rooms which . . . were faultily constructed and ugly. The first thing the Sisters did was to pull down the ugly, badly constructed wing and erect more commodious and less unsightly buildings." Judging by the old photographs which show Dr. Barrett's wing of dormitories and servants' quarters west of the Colonnade, "ugly" seems rather too strong a word to apply to it. But something was undoubtedly wrong with its construction; in 1906 a subsidence on the north side left the roof unsupported. The whole building had to be hastily evacuated and demolished; and, while a new and enlarged dormitory block was being put up on the site, the girls slept in the mansion.

The Daughters of the Cross had no need of a contretemps like this to give them architectural opportunities. They were already engaged on an extensive building and redevelopment programme which, in the end, was to sweep away all the 18th century domestic ancillaries. But what they had found on the site could not possibly have been made to provide suitable accommodation for all the needs of the Convent and its schools. The chapel in the Waterhouse would have been a very inconveniently situated place of worship for a community based on the mansion and having to attend services at least three times a day, the first at 5.30 a.m. and the last at 9 p.m. So, to begin with, the Sisters used Dr. Barrett's dining hall for services, adding a chancel to its south end. But by 1900 the present church had been erected on the western outskirts of the old Carleton "back yard", necessitating only the demolition of some old sheds and a barn or two. (The dovecote was still standing at this time.) A year earlier, one of the most pressing needs, a Novitiate, had been built on the east side of the Carleton back yard; and five years afterwards, actually on part of that area, construction of a Professed House began. (By 1901 there were already 50 Sisters and 30 Novices to accommodate.) Quarters for the 'Province' had also to be provided, and, in the course of all these building operations, the ancient dovecote disappeared. It may well have been in poor repair by now, as doves had long since ceased to be part of the well-off Englishman's diet.

While all this work was going on for conventual purposes, the schools were expanding too, and requiring additional premises. Very soon after the Sisters had come to Carshalton they had started a day preparatory school in the Waterhouse for fee-paying pupils of both sexes. Then, in 1903, they substituted for a barn on the west side of the Fellowes' stable block, a new building which they named St. Aloysius House. This provided dormitories and other rooms for a preparatory school for boy boarders who shared lessons with the day children in the 'Tower School'. It was in 1903 also that Carshalton House was given the very up-to-date amenity of electricity; and it stayed well up with the times when it acquired the telephone in 1907.

The 'Aloysians' were never numerous, but they made their contribution to the school magazine: a 1911 issue, for instance, contained a letter from an eleven year old boarder whose Easter holiday had been spent in the school "very merrily . . . out in the grounds nearly all day". A thrush's nest had been discovered and much entertainment obtained out of watching the progress of the brood from egg to feathered but tailless avian adolescence. A few years later *The Philomena* was recording the death of some of these young lads on the battlefields of the First World War.

St. Philomena's itself, the girls' boarding school, had at first taken over the class-rooms which Dr. Barrett's pupils had used and which had once housed horses and carriages. The assembly hall, called St. Philip's Hall, was actually the old coach-house and still retained its two large carriage doors opening on to the stable yard — which was called the 'quad' and served as the girls' playground. Asphalted over by 1905 it is still called the 'quad' and is not easily imaginable now as a once stony stable yard. The ingenious building conversion which fronted it — and would have greatly surprised Sir John Fellowes — was not to last much longer. In 1909 a complete demolition and rebuilding of the stable block was begun, and, two years later, most of the present school buildings on the west side of the carriage drive were completed. Nothing of the 18th century now remained in this area, but Dr. Barrett's dining room was incorporated in the new fabric at its northern end, and, as already mentioned, a fragment of The Old Farm was preserved in the new walls.

Even this massive constructional operation did not enable the Sisters to meet all the demands for accommodation made by their continually expanding schools. The boys' boarding school seems to have been given up round about 1912, which meant that the rooms in St. Aloysius House could be added to St. Philomena's. But a more drastic solution had to be found for the problems of the

Tower School, which still took day boys up to the age of 8 and was beginning to make the Waterhouse metaphorically bulge at the seams. In 1911 an entirely new building for day pupils was put up in West Street and named St. Joseph's. (The site was part of the old 'Coulsons' field which still remained with Carshalton House.) Even this eventually proved too small as the number of pupils wishing to attend the day school kept on increasing. But, as an article in *The Philomena* explained in 1920, to enlarge the building would have taken a long time "especially in these days of short hours and frequent strikes". (It is evidently a mistake to regard the 'British disease' as a post-*Second* World War epidemic.) The problem was solved by transferring the St. Joseph's pupils aged from 4 to 10 (some 50 in number) back to the Waterhouse.

A Bazaar, at which one of the attractions was "ten minute drives in a large motor-car", raised £70 towards the contractors' bills. For there had been a sad deterioration in the condition of the Waterhouse. To quote again from the 1920 article, "repairs were badly needed and, as the War was raging, it was impossible to have them done. The rain came through the roof in torrents, the walls were spoiled; everything of any use had to be taken away, and desolation reigned." The writer continued: "This Summer, however, the workmen started on what to the uninitiated might have seemed a hopeless task. They took off the two-hundred-year-old roof and made a new one; they skinned the old decaying wood from the walls *[alas, that that had become necessary!]*; the little dark room at the end *[presumably the Fellowes dressing room]* was made bright and airy by a large new window. Gas radiators were placed in every room . . . . Three of the rooms are painted in a delicate eau de Nil colour; the room with the tiles *[the bathroom]* is blue to match the tiles, and all four look wonderfully pretty and comfortable."

The Hermitage could not be adapted to scholastic uses, but it also underwent a transformation in 1920. Under the heading "Ecce Homo" *The Philomena* reported its new role in the following terms: "The old boats have disappeared; the landing-stage is gone; nothing now blocks the dark passage to the inner cave — that gloomy, dim dungeon with its earthen floor and air of mystery. It is no gloomy dungeon now. The old grating in the roof has been replaced by a covering of amber-coloured glass; the rough walls have been plastered over, and the mud floor is covered with tiles. A second opening has been made into the outer cave, and the whole forms a little oratory, a little home of prayer — for the Master of the House has taken possession of the cave . . . . He is seated there, as the Man of Sorrows, with thorn-crowned head and the reed for sceptre held in His fast-bound hands." But nowadays 'Danger' notices outside the Hermitage warn that prayer inside might be too late.

While all these changes were being made in the ancillary buildings of Carshalton House the mansion stayed pretty much as it was when the Daughters of the Cross took it over. The Oak Room and the Painted Parlour had, early on, been used as school dining rooms, but later the mansion was reserved for the Sisters. They continued to use the domestic offices in the basement, but a new bakery and a new laundry were built. (There was not much left now of the old Carleton back yard, which had, long since, been renamed 'the drying ground'). Some changes were made, too, in the Colonnade after the rebuilding of the dormitory wing. The conservatory which the Sale Catalogue of 1888 located over the Colonnade had first become the 'Blue Verandah', forming a link between the

Two pictures showing the pupils of St. Philomena's taking exercise, c.1912.

school sleeping quarters and the first floor of the mansion, and so helping super-vision at night. Then, in 1920, the Blue Verandah was re-roofed and turned into the Blue Room, "the dining-hall of our little ones", while a new passage was con-structed behind it to lead from the mansion to the dormitory and infirmary block (which, itself, acquired five additional bathrooms at the same time). The passing of the conservatory which the *Victoria County History* had found "forming the principal entrance" does not seem to have been recorded. But the "broad circular flight of stone steps" which had for long provided the main access to the house was presumably removed for transfer to the swimming bath when that was built in 1909. Anyway, the present-day visitor enters the mansion by some very modest steps leading to a very modest door in the west end of the filled-in Colonnade, which is now all one with the Entrance Hall.

The four schools run by the Daughters of the Cross (with some secular help on the teaching staffs) continued to function in their separate buildings until 1932. In that year an amalgamation took place which probably reflected what was happening nationally in the field of education. Boarding schools were declining somewhat in popularity as the number of excellent day secondary schools steadily increased, and many of the latter had waiting lists of prospective pupils. This seems to have been what accounted for the merger, in 1932, of the senior St. Joseph's girls and all the St. Philomena's pupils in a new school which used the premises of the latter. The junior day girls remained in the West Street building, and the Waterhouse retained its Kindergarten role.

Local patriotisms were outraged by this undoubtedly very sensible solution of an accommodation problem, and naming the new combined establishment 'Carshalton House Collegiate School' did little to reconcile either set of girls to the loss of their former identity. A number of the boarders left, and, for a time, those who remained kept aloof from the day girls. But a new headmistress, Sister Mary Alban, eventually managed to weld the new school into a unity. One diffi-culty facing her she overcame by a particularly bold stroke of genius. Both St. Philomena's and St. Joseph's had fielded strongly supported hockey teams, but now lacrosse instead of hockey was decreed to be the school game.

An advertising brochure of the Carshalton House Collegiate School simply states that it was "formerly known as St. Philomena's College" and since 1918 had "been on the Board of Education list of Approved Schools" – which did not mean then what it does now. In fact, the School was said to be "for the daughters of professional men and Government officials at home and abroad", but it offered also a special course in English for Foreign Students. A Secretarial Course provi-ded tuition in Shorthand, Typewriting, English and Book-keeping; and there was, too, a Domestic Course for those who wished "to learn how to cook and look after a house" – which meant learning about Dressmaking, Embroidery, Cookery, Housecraft, Home Nursing, Hygiene and First Aid. But all pupils had first to take the normal school subjects. Twenty-nine pounds a term was the charge made for boarders, and, unless extra subjects were taken, parents had little more to pay, because it was a rule that "No sweets or other eatables may be kept privately" and, for pocket money, "A sum of about £1 (Juniors) to £2 (Senior forms) is ample for the needs of the term."

Just as the Collegiate School was going along smoothly with past frictions eliminated, the Second World War broke out and upset everything in quite a different way. During that five-year ordeal, Carshalton House, like a well-advertised establishment of a very dissimilar kind, never closed; but, when the 'blitz' of 1940 struck London, the number of pupils went down to 89 — which included a baker's dozen from the preparatory school. The West Street premises had to be evacuated because they could offer no protection against bombs, and Edward Carleton's basement was now made to serve as an air-raid shelter. Luckily, its strength was never tested to the utmost, but there is no reason to doubt that this early 18th century foundation would have withstood the collapse of the whole building on it. The 32 remaining boarders slept in the basement, and the whole school retired there during air raids, getting on with lessons as normally as possible. By good fortune, only the laundry suffered a direct hit (and had to be rebuilt), but much non-structural damage, including shattered windows, was done, by the bursting of bombs in the vicinity, to most of the buildings in the grounds of Carshalton House. And, when the flying bombs began to fall, still more children were removed from the district, with the result that, by July 1944, there were only 50 pupils left in the school.

All this information about happenings in the 1930s and 1940s has been obtained from a brief history of the schools which was written for the 80th birthday of *Philomena* (it had dropped *'The'* by then). This also recounts that the flags and bunting used to celebrate V.E. Day had been stored in the "turkey shed". Could that possibly have been the one mentioned in the 1839 Sale Catalogue? The Daughters of the Cross seem unlikely to have built special accommodation for turkeys — though they did, for quite a long while, keep poultry.

Two years after peace was restored to the country, the Carshalton House Collegiate School became 'St. Philomena's' again — which was what a lot of people had never ceased to call it. Then, in 1960, Rome announced that the child saint whose tomb was believed to have been discovered in St. Priscilla's catacomb was not an authentic martyr. Fortunately, there were other St. Philomenas in the calendar of saints, and one from Hyrcana, whose feast day is on the 5th July, was eventually adopted as the patroness of Carshalton House's school.

In the meantime another era of building had begun on the site. New science laboratories came into existence; additional class-rooms were constructed for the Senior School — and their number was further added to when the boarding school closed, making dormitories available for exercising the juvenile mind instead of resting it. Near the 18th century Waterhouse, a new building, very 20th century in style, was put up to house the old St. Joseph's Junior School; and the West Street premises later took the younger children from St. Mary's, thereby losing the old name of St. Joseph's and becoming an additional St. Mary's. Finally, in 1973, a modern gymnasium was added to the amenities of St. Philomena's, and the one, built about 1904, which, in its time, had offered all the most up-to-date facilities for physical education, was converted into a second Domestic Science kitchen.

But improvements in the physical surroundings of the scholars have had only minor effects in comparison with non-material changes which have taken place in St. Philomena's since the ending of the Second World War. The school could not isolate itself from the social and political movements which have revolutionised the whole course and purpose of education in England. The philosophy which lies behind these modern developments is still the subject of often fierce controversy, and is not appropriate for discussion in a book which is concerned with the past. All that need be said here about the matter is that St. Philomena's ceased to be an 'independent' school and became one of the Borough's 'comprehensive' schools, with over 700 pupils, all of them day scholars and none of them fee-paying.

What the Daughters of the Cross passed on to the general public was the result of religious inspiration, but, simply from a mundane point of view, it was a remarkable achievement. Within the span of a human lifetime they had transformed a derelict preparatory school with makeshift class-rooms into an educational complex catering for all ages of children in purpose-built accommodation equipped with all the usual modern teaching aids. And all this had been done without the benefit of any legislation to make women the equals of men.

The rest of the Carshalton House site still remains in the possession of the Daughters of the Cross. In the early years of this century the *Victoria County History* said that "In spite of its many occupants the house itself has been little disturbed and stands to-day in practically the same condition as when erected." And much the same can still be said of it. This is really very remarkable, considering that the place never became a family possession passing from father to son, but had a continual succession of occupiers, few of whom lived in it for even ten years and none − except for the Daughters of the Cross − for as long as thirty years.

All the same, during the course of nearly three hundred years, alterations in the use made of parts of the premises have resulted in blocked-up doorways, steps which seem to lead nowhere, and apparently sealed-off nooks and crannies. From these there have inevitably sprung stories of secret passages, openings operated by concealed springs and, of course, ghosts. A number of alleged spooky happenings have been related to Sister Pauline Stevens, but I think she puts as little credence in their supernatural origin as I do. The most unusual apparition is one spoken of − but not, I fancy, believed in − by Charles Barrett. The story in his notes is that Sir John Fellowes, enraged by the importunities of a tax collector, threw him downstairs with such force that he broke his neck; and, ever after, the staircase was haunted by the shade of a conscientious government servant seeking settlement of a debt due to the Crown. (If my theory is correct he ought now to be appearing in mid-air where there are no stairs.) Actually, Edward Carleton's name could more plausibly have been attached to this tale; he might well have had a Customs officer calling on him for unpaid tobacco duty. But, as a matter of cold, hard fact, there is not a scrap of evidence that any foul deed of any kind has ever been done within the precincts of Carshalton House. Nevertheless, the romantic appeal of ghost stories will ensure that the place never lacks these standard appurtenances of an ancient mansion. The youthful imagination of the present pupils of the school has already created an entirely new spectre − "the gray lady of the Waterhouse". In truth, the building does look as if it ought to be haunted; and, to the modern eye, its original very utilitarian purposes are not immediately apparent. But the fact is that no gray lady would have found any occupation in it unless she was a bath attendant, or a pump-house assistant − or, perhaps, the gardener's wife, helping in the orangery.

It is much to be hoped that the Waterhouse will long remain to enhance the appearance both of West Street and the grounds of Carshalton House. But the lake which once powered it will not reappear unless expensive water engineering is undertaken. Costly too might be the repairs necessary if the Hermitage beside the lake is not to turn from a mock ruin into a real one. No expenditure of money, though, could bring back the old stable block, the dovecote and the 18th century domestic offices outside the main building. Nevertheless, enough remains of the Carleton-Fellowes creation to make Carshalton House a very remarkable survival from the past, offering some unique architectural features and giving a very good idea of how the well-off lived in the time of Queen Anne and George I. It has a Grade 2 rating as a house of historic interest worthy of preservation; but a case could be made for its being classified as Grade 1, i.e. one of those buildings "of such importance that their destruction should in no case be allowed".

APPENDIX

Some notes on properties which went with Carshalton House

THE GROUNDS

No document which has come down to us gives any idea of the extent of the land which constituted the precincts of The Old Farm. But property deeds and the Court Rolls do provide some information about various 'closes' which were eventually incorporated into the grounds of Carshalton House and, after Fellowes had built his boundary wall, had to be sold with the mansion and ceased to be mentioned by their old names in conveyances.

The key to the location of those old additions to the original 'grounds' of The Old Farm would seem to be a frequently mentioned close whose name appears in many forms, the earliest surviving of which is "Amners Earth or Ammes Ace". It is so designated in the 1716 conveyance of freeholds to Sir John Fellowes, which also describes it as an enclosed orchard, containing 3 acres, to the north of the house. It is, however, quite likely that this description was copied — or miscopied — from an earlier conveyance which related to The Old Farm; and that building, judging by the position of the fragment of old chalk and flint wall, lay well to the south of Carshalton House. Even so, 'A . . . A . . .' cannot have been entirely to the north of the house if the 1656 conveyance of 'Hill Close' to Spencer Dallyson was correctly worded. That had the 1½ acre of Hill Close abutting on "Ames Ace" to the south and on The Old Farm to the north — an impossibility if 'A . . . A . . .' was to the north of the house.

Some idea of the truth of the matter is obtainable from an analysis of other documentary evidence. When Dallyson died in 1691 the Court Rolls reported 'Hilly Close' to be in the occupation of Edward Carleton. Dallyson's heir was "not known", but it was mentioned that Theodosia Arden (who had died in 1686) was his sister. If she was his heiress the property might well have come to Thomas Arden and, in that way, have formed part of Carleton's purchase of Arden's former estate.

In 1657 Dixye Longe (then living in The Old Farm) had been accused of stopping up "a common footway leading through a close called Hill Close from the West Street towards Sutton". This seems to be identical with the "Way leading from the West Street by The Old Farm to the Field Gate" which is mentioned in the Court Rolls for 1661. The common fields must have been bordered by

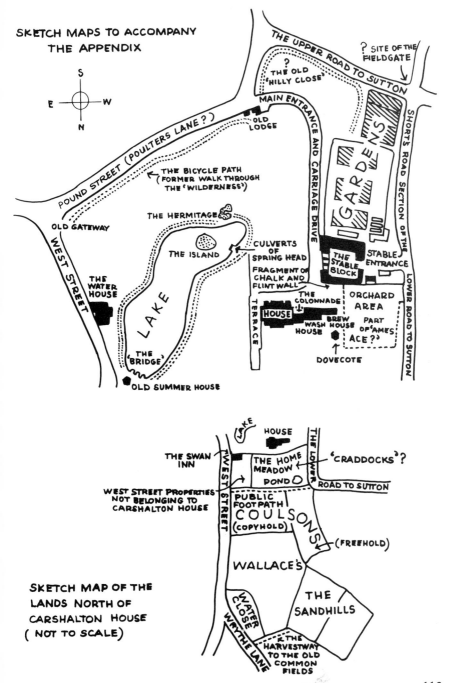

SKETCH MAPS TO ACCOMPANY
THE APPENDIX

S
E · · · W
N

THE UPPER ROAD TO SUTTON

? SITE OF THE FIELDGATE

?
THE OLD 'HILLY CLOSE'

MAIN ENTRANCE

POUND STREET (POULTERS LANE ?)

OLD LODGE

GARDENS

SHORTS ROAD SECTION OF THE

THE BICYCLE PATH
(FORMER WALK THROUGH
THE 'WILDERNESS')

THE HERMITAGE

OLD GATEWAY

MAIN ENTRANCE AND CARRIAGE DRIVE

THE ISLAND

CULVERTS OF SPRING HEAD

STABLE ENTRANCE

THE STABLE BLOCK

WEST STREET

THE WATER HOUSE

LAKE

FRAGMENT OF CHALK AND FLINT WALL

THE COLONNADE

HOUSE

TERRACE

BREW WASH HOUSE HOUSE

ORCHARD AREA

PART OF 'AMES ACE'?

LOWER ROAD TO SUTTON

THE 'BRIDGE'

DOVECOTE

OLD SUMMER HOUSE

LAKE

HOUSE

THE SWAN INN

WEST STREET

THE HOME MEADOW

THE LOWER

'CRADDOCKS'?

POND

ROAD TO SUTTON

WEST STREET PROPERTIES NOT BELONGING TO CARSHALTON HOUSE

PUBLIC FOOT PATH

COULSONS
(COPYHOLD)

(FREEHOLD)

WALLACE'S

WATER CLOSE

THE SANDHILLS

SKETCH MAP OF THE LANDS NORTH OF CARSHALTON HOUSE
(NOT TO SCALE)

WRYTHE LANE

THE HARVESTWAY TO THE OLD COMMON FIELDS

113

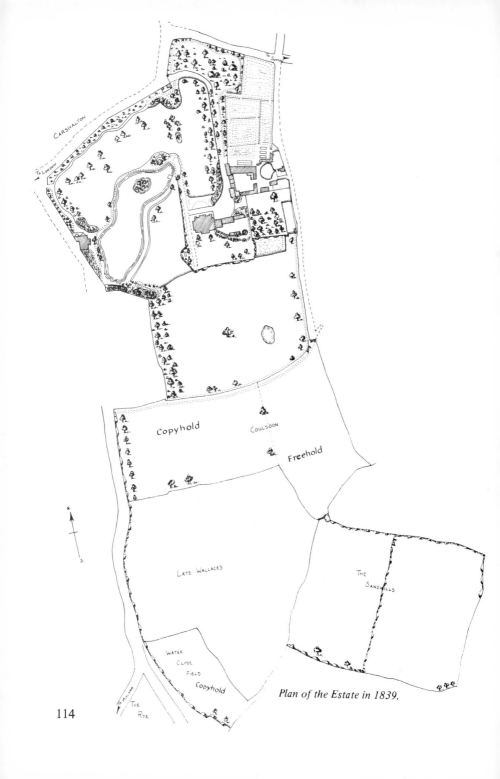

CARSHALTON

To London

To Sutton

Copyhold

COULSDON

Freehold

N

S.

LATE WALLACE'S

THE SANDHILLS

WATER CLOSE FIELD Copyhold

To Mitcham

THE RYE

Plan of the Estate in 1839.

114

fenced or hedged enclosures, so that public access to the common property would have been obtainable only by roads across which there probably existed gates to keep animals either in or out. On this basis the 'Field Gate' in question would have been across the road to Sutton, most likely by the modern Short's Road, beyond which the common fields began. The south boundary of the Carshalton House estate is given in the 1839 sale catalogue as "in part by the road called Poulter's Lane leading from Carshalton to Sutton, and in part by the road from Carshalton to the Common Field Gate and to London". This corresponds with the suggested location of the Field Gate if Poulter's Lane was the current name for the present Pound Street, and using the turnpike road at Sutton was the generally accepted way of getting to London.

The Court Rolls, when recording the transfer of Hill Close in 1656, gave its boundary on the east as "Spring Close", and on the west as "the footway leading from Carshalton towards Sutton". The footway from West Street cannot have been that boundary because it ran *through* Hill Close. The only possible footway on the west was what is now Short's Road. By 1732 it had evidently become a road, but it was still described as leading to Sutton when, in that year, Coulson Fellowes sold to Samuel Swinfen, *inter alia*, a piece of land "abutting on a close called Amners Earth alias Ambs Ace, and then including the road leading from Carshalton to Sutton called the Lower Road (*of which Short's Road was an indistinguishable part*) abutting on the lands of Mr. Philip Yorke (*later Lord Hardwicke*), and sometime since the lands of Sir John Fellowes, to the east". Furthermore, in 1787, land called "Challmer's piece, part of the common lands" was described in a conveyance to Samuel Long as "abutting east on Lower Road and enclosed land of Theodore Henry Broadhead (*the current owner of Carshalton House*), then used as a garden, formerly known by the name of Amners Earth or Ambs Ace".

It is clear from all this that a mistake was made in the Court Rolls in 1656 when Hill Close was described as abutting on Ames Ace to the south. 'A . . . A . . .' had become part of Broadhead's garden by 1787, and the 1839 estate map shows the main kitchen gardens of the house lying south of the stable block (at the north east corner of which was the fragment of chalk and flint wall). It is conceivable that the Fellowes' stables were built on part of 'A . . . A . . .' and its original 3 acre orchard extended both north and south of The Old Farm, with the major portion lying to the north of that building. (On the 1839 map there appears to be an orchard indicated due west of the Carshalton House mansion.) On that basis the phraseology of the 1716 conveyance to Fellowes might be justified, and the geography would be understandable if Hill Close was bounded on the *north* by both The Old Farm and 'A . . . A . . .', the latter to the west and the former to the east. These are, admittedly, suppositions, but they do make sense of the documents and of the footway stoppage. If one takes all the words used as factually true one is forced to equate north with south.

There is another indication that Hill Close occupied the south west corner of the present Carshalton House grounds. In the 1716 conveyance of freeholds to Fellowes, Chalkhill, Spring Close, Roomes and the Little Pightle are said to have been laid together and called "the Grove Wilderness or Spring". This Spring Close must surely be identical with the one mentioned as forming the eastern boundary of Hill Close, and "Chalkhill" is presumably another name for the latter. (If, as seems likely, Spring Close was named from the springhead of the lake, it would lie to the east of a Hill Close which occupied the south west part of the estate). One can assume that the closes would be listed in the conveyance in some sort of topographical order, and the description in the conveyance of the copyhold part of 'Roomes' fits in with this. It abutted on the Vicarage House to the east and the Horse Pond to the west. This wording was probably copied from the Court Rolls and may well have related to the position as it was when the 'Arundel' map was drawn. Assuming that, as shown thereon, West Street did not reach as far as Pound Street, and that the Vicarage House was the present Old Rectory, the lands of the latter would have met those of Carshalton House. It would probably be impossible now to identify the 'Horse Pond' because it is pretty clear that the lay-out of Carshalton's waters was once very different from what it became later on in the 18th century. (The whole question is, to some extent, bound up with the making of the foot causeway alongside the ford through the water at the end of West Street; that foot causeway, if it had existed in 1716, would surely have been an obvious feature to mention as a boundary.)

If the 'Grove Wilderness' has, so far, been correctly identified geographically, it corresponds with the area known as 'the Wilderness' early in this century — i.e. the whole southern border of the estate. But what, from the wording of the 1716 conveyance, seems to have also been regarded as part of the Grove Wilderness — a close called Craddocks — is puzzling because, on the boundaries assigned to it, it could not have adjoined any of the other constituents of this feature of the estate. (Perhaps a 'Wilderness' in that connection simply meant, to the early 18th century, land which was neither cultivated nor grazed?) Craddocks is first mentioned in the Court Rolls for 1446 when it was a toft with garden and appurtenances, with which there also went 2 adjoining acres in "the west field of Kersalton"; it lay between "lands called Kenwardesle" (the land which went with The Old Farm) on two sides, and had Westmead to the north. In 1530 the Court Rolls described Craddocks as "a croft with water there", together with 2 acres at the southern end of Westmead. And, in a list of old land deeds in the Guildford Record Office, there is mention of one which recorded the transfer in 1660 of "a pasture called Craddocks lately planted with cherry trees" from John Pollard of St. Clement Danes to "Dixy Long of Carshalton". The latter's Carshalton property passed from his widow to her second husband, Thomas Arden, from him to Edward Carleton and then to Sir John Fellowes.

As Craddocks was between the grounds of The Old Farm and Westmead — i.e. on the north side of the house — it could not have adjoined the eastern end of a Grove Wilderness which ran alongside Pound Street, and 'A . . . A . . .' would have separated it from the western end of that area. Since it is mentioned as having water attached to it, the most likely site of Craddocks is the western part of what came to be called the "Home meadow" of Carshalton House, in which old estate maps show a sizeable pond. (See the plan on page 113).

One further plot of land mentioned in the 1716 conveyance of freeholds to Sir John Fellowes seems to have formed part of the grounds both of The Old Farm and Carshalton House. It was 2 acres of pasture called Stockbridge, "now Stockbridge Orchard with barn." In 1656 the Court Rolls had reported the admission of Dixey Longe as the owner of this copyhold, and also his alleged stopping up of "a common footway leading through Stockbridge to ye Fieldgate" together

116

with "a Cartway leading without ye hedge from West Street to ye Common feild"). It seems likely that these rights of way ran from the northern end of West Street towards Carshalton Road in the vicinity of Short's Road, and Stockbridge, accordingly, would have been to the north of the mansion. It is not separately named in later Carshalton House deeds and presumably just became merged in the grounds.

COULSONS AND WA(L)TERS

The Court Rolls record that, in 1446, Adam Paris took over a toft called Colswayns with 4 acres of land. In those village annals it is also noted that, in 1483, William and Anne Say were in possession of a croft called Colswaynes containing one acre. Then in 1539 an entry was made concerning the transfer by John Rychbelle to his married daughter, Elizabeth Bolton, of a close called Colswaynes, a toft and one acre "formerly Sayes" and a plot of land called Walters. Thirty-two years later Elizabeth Ache (who may have been Rychbelle's re-married daughter) disposed of "Coleswaynes" and Walters, together with "a croft and four acres formerly Says". (It cannot be taken for granted that the manorial scribes never made a mistake; moreover, like the O.E.D., they made little distinction between a toft and a croft.) In 1639 "a close called Coulsden" together with Hilly Close (see page 113) and 5½ acres in Westmead passed to John Wood with his acquisition of "a moiety of the Manor of Kinnersley". And, in 1661, John Wood, like John Rychbelle in the previous century, settled land on his married daughter. She, Ann Waterman, received from him, *inter alia*, 8 acres called Coulsons and "a close called Waters", containing 1½ acre "in the Rythe by the West Lands". Mrs. Waterman's son and heir, Christopher, in 1684, sold all his property in Carshalton to Edward Carleton; it included "8 acres called Coulsons and a small close called Walters". Naturally, then, Walters and "Coulson or Coulsdon" appear in the 1716 conveyance of Carleton copyholds to Sir John Fellowes.

Those two closes, together with the land in between them, went with Carshalton House for well over a hundred years. This was quite understandable, because they formed a natural geographical addition to the mansion's grounds. Their respective locations are established by old estate maps, one of which dates from the 1839 auction of the premises. (See the sketch plan on page 113.) At that time "Coulsdon" was described as "a valuable meadow formerly in 2 or 3 closes ... divided merely by a sunk fence on the north side of the paddock [the 'Home meadow'] , with frontage on the road leading from the village to the Rye Common and to Mitcham." (But the public footpath which runs from West Street to Westmead Corner, between 'Coulsons' and the grounds of the mansion, is shown on the estate map.) The 8 acres which "Coulsons" had been estimated to contain in 1661 had apparently been more accurately measured since; the area of "Coulsdon" in 1839 was put at 9 acres, 3 roods and 20 poles. Furthermore, only 5 acres, 1 rood and 3 poles were now copyhold, the remainder, to the west, being freehold. With "Coulsdon" there also went, in the 1839 sale – in addition to land called "Wallace's" (see page 114) – "Water Close Field", a copyhold containing 1 acre, 3 roods and 36 poles, bordering the present Wrythe Lane. (In 1586 the Court Rolls had recorded that "the customary Harvestway" through this area into the common fields "was to be laid open for carts and carriages, the passers into the same shutting the gates". That "Harvestway", then a private lane, was still shown on 19th century maps.)

Coulsons – or Coulsdon – stayed with Carshalton House until the South London Railway was extended to Sutton, via Carshalton, in 1868. The embanked track of that modern enterprise cut right through this medieval close, leaving only a small meadow on the Carshalton House side. The larger portion was bought by Mr. Jackson, a London solicitor who lived in Beechwood Lodge at the east end of West Street Lane. But this was only a revenue producing investment for Mr. Jackson; the land was actually used by the Shorts as an extension of the dairy farm they worked on Westmead land. After the First World War the Westmead Farm was 'developed' as a housing estate with roads named after British poets. At the same time 'Coulsons' and 'Wallaces' also had houses built on them, but only one new road was needed to accommodate those. It was given the name of Colston Avenue, perpetuating a final variation of the medieval 'Colswayns'.

The remnant of the old close south of the railway line still goes with Carshalton House. In the early years of their occupation of the premises, the Daughters of the Cross used it as pasture for the cows they then kept; but later they built on its West Street frontage St. Joseph's High School for Girls, which now serves as an extension of St. Mary's Primary School. On the opposite side of West Street the house called 'Colstonfields' has been demolished to make space for a car park for 'The Hope'; so only the road now acts as a reminder of the past of this area of Carshalton.

SHEPHERDS CLOSES ALIAS HEDGES LAND ALIAS WALLACE'S

In the Surrey Record Office's collection of deeds relating to Samuel Long's estate there are a number of references to "Shepherds Closes containing 14 acres and 15½ acres in the common fields". The earliest conveyance cited under this heading is one to Edward Carleton dated the 15th December 1698, the vendors being Thomas and John Best. The land in question passed with the rest of the Carleton estate to Sir John Fellowes and is specified in the 1716 conveyance of freeholds to him as "3 closes of land now divided into 4 closes, called Shepherds Closes or Hedges Land", a pasture of 14 acres "formerly occupied by George Hawkins"; with this there went "Parcels of land lying dispersedly in the Common Fields on both sides of the road from Carshalton between the pits called Sutton Chalk Pits in or near Westmead, Westmead Corner, Benhill Shott alias Westmead Shott, Barrowes Hedge Shott, Stoneheaps and Banstead Way". The total acreage of these "parcels" was 15½, of which 3 were on the south and 12½ on the north side of the road.

In 1732 Coulson Fellowes sold these 29½ acres, together with other parts of his Carshalton inheritance, to Samuel Swinfen. The clerk who drew up the conveyance copied all the details faithfully from the 1716 one, except that, probably through a misreading, he made Benhill into Penhill. Samuel Swinfen's heir was Thomas Ball, who, in 1763, settled extensive Carshalton holdings on his prospective bride; but there is no mention of "Shepherds Closes" or "Hedges land" in the deed. Numerous pieces of land in the common fields are named, but it is impossible to identify their exact location with any certainty. The inference would seem to be that Shepherds Closes had been sold before 1763, possibly with the common land which had gone with it in 1732.

Sister Pauline Stevens found in the present deeds of Carshalton House a reference to land, which once went with it, called "Wallace's". This contained 12 acres, 2 roods and 8 poles and was stated to have been formerly two pieces of land called "the Near Seven Acres" and "the Far Seven Acres", which, either in part or whole were known as "Hedges Mead". The association of 14 acres with that latter name strongly suggests that this holding was the one time Shepherds Closes. It was certainly one which could be expected to go with Carshalton House; for "Wallace's" northern and eastern boundaries were given as "Water Close Field" and "a lane leading from the West End of West Street to the Rye or Rith", while the estate map drawn at the time of the 1839 sale of Carshalton House shows a large field labelled "late Wallace's" in between Coulsons and Water Close with a frontage on West Street. (On its north west side were two meadows called "Sandhills" which also went with Carshalton House.) It seems likely that Shepherds Closes alias Hedges Land was bought by Samuel Wallace, who was Carshalton's surgeon in the second half of the 18th century, and later re-acquired for Carshalton House by William Foster Reynolds, the owner of the mansion from 1816 until his death in 1838.

LAND ADJOINING MINNUMS

Included in the freehold properties acquired by Sir John Fellowes from Edward Carleton's estate was one which abutted "on a close called Minnums to the south, on the highway to the north, on Widow Overy's land to the east, and on late Mr. Surman's land on the west, formerly in the tenure of Nicholas Hickson, late of John Hickson", to quote from the conveyance of 1716. The deeds of Samuel Long's estate, now in the Surrey Record Office, refer to this holding as "a messuage and one acre of land abutting on a close called Minnums on the south side of the highway at Carshalton", which, in 1686, had been sold by Allen Avery to William Horton. Those deeds show also that, in 1732, Coulson Fellowes, who ultimately inherited Sir John's property, sold to Samuel Swinfen "two several messuages or tenements, with Barn, garden and one acre of land with trees thereon, and appurtenances in Carshalton, abutting on a Cross *[clearly a copyist's error for 'Close']* called Minnums to the south, on the highway to the north, on the late Mr. Overie's estate *['East' is omitted here]*, and the late Mr. Surman's land to the west, theretofore in the tenure of Nicholas Hickson."

The situation of this property is established by the conjunction of its being on the main Carshalton highway and also immediately to the west of land belonging to the Overys. This family carried on a blacksmith's, wheelwright's and coach builder's business in Carshalton during the 17th and 18th centuries, and its premises were on the south side of Pound Street roughly opposite West Street. As far back as 1446 the Court Rolls had recorded that Adam Popelote was fined 20 pence for not repairing his tenement. His name was also spelled Popletoes, and, a century later, there is mention in the Court Rolls of "an orchard in the south part of the tenement called Pupletts". Then, in 1682, "Richard Overy, son and heir of Mary Overy" was admitted to possession of "a tenement and ½ acre called Pupletts". However, in the middle of the 18th century, the Masperos took over the Overys' business, and, in the middle of the 19th century they sold part of the Pound Street holding to James Mellon Bickford, who was, at one time or another, master of Carshalton's National School, its rate collector, and the secretary of its Gas Company. What he acquired was a house called 'The Pulpits' and four adjoining 'Hereditaments' to the east of it. The Masperos kept the remainder of the property extending further eastwards to the present Carshalton Park Road, which was then just a 'yard' off the main street.

The houses owned by the Masperos have all vanished and their site is now occupied by a large garage; but Mr. Bickford's acquisitions still stand, though the two next to 'The Pulpits' have recently been badly damaged by a fire. In the late 19th century 'The Pulpits' became the 'Regent Dining Rooms', but it has since housed businesses of a different kind. It is unlikely that the building stands exactly where Adam Popelote's decaying tenement did in the 15th century, because it is right up against the western boundary of its land. On the other side of that boundary its neighbour, during the 18th and 19th centuries, had been 'The Pound House', owned and occupied by the Wallaces, Carshalton's surgeons for over a hundred years. Their estate was sold in the early 1900s, the mansion was demolished, and the present Wallace Crescent was formed out of its grounds. It is clear that this land, like the grounds of many of Carshalton's big houses, had been an amalgamation of a number of medieval 'closes'; and one of those must have been 'Minnums', while another was the Avery/Carleton/Fellowes holding which had 'Minnums' to the south, the Overys' land to the east and the main road to the north. (The history of the site shows, incidentally, that Pound Street is a very old road and the inhabitants of Carshalton were not obliged to use Crooked Lane if they wanted to get to Sutton.)

Before the high brick walls of Carshalton House and The Pound House were built, it would have been quite natural and convenient for a property owner to have had land on each side of Pound Street. But, after Sir John Fellowes had put an impassable barrier all along the southern boundary of his grounds, there was no reason to retain with the estate the holding next to 'Minnums'. After its sale in 1732 by Coulson Fellowes to Samuel Swinfen it came eventually to the latter's heir, Thomas Ball. But this particular possession was not mentioned in the marriage settlement Thomas Ball made, which seems to have included all his Carshalton property at that date, 1763. In all probability it had already been bought by the Wallaces; and that would account for references Sister Pauline Stevens has come across to property deeds which indicate that land belonging to 'The Pound House' once went with Carshalton House. By the middle of the 19th century the Wallace family did, in fact, own two substantial houses in Pound Street, but it is extremely unlikely that they were the same two 'messuages' which went with the land next to 'Minnums' when Coulson Fellowes sold it in 1732.

THE CHALK PIT

In this century, along the bottom of an ancient chalk pit, houses have been built on each side of a new road called Rossdale which runs southwards off Westmead Road (the former Lower Road to Sutton) near its eastern end. A steep bank making Rossdale a cul-de-sac marks where quarrying operations had to cease, otherwise the stability of Carshalton Road would have been threatened. To the west, Highfield Road (the name is meaningful) looks down on its neighbour from the edge of the former chalk pit. The land hereabouts and the quarry itself once belonged to Carshalton House. When that property was auctioned in 1839 the lots included "III. 1 acre of copyhold in Carshalton Common Fields, known as Footpath Acre, near the Old Chalk Pit. The footway from Carshalton to Sutton leads through it. IV. Approximately 1 acre in the Common Fields known as Inn Peartree, subject to the same footpath. V. 1 acre (or piece) in the Common Fields known as the Old Chalk Pit." The actual area given for these 'acres' was, in each case, considerably less, indicating, presumably, the extent to which, over the centuries, the quarry had eaten into the surrounding land.

It is difficult to make a precise identification of Lots III, IV and V with lands mentioned in old deeds, but one of the freeholds in question may have figured in the 1716 conveyance to Sir John Fellowes of Edward Carleton's estate as "Chalk pit or piece of ground and its borders, part of a 4 acre shott formerly of Allen Avery, abutting north on Sutton footway and north and south on the ploughed lands of the shott. The breadth of the chalk pit is the breadth of the 4 acre shott." When this land was sold by Coulson Fellowes to Samuel Swinfen in 1732 it was described as "Chalk pit, part of a 4 acre shott, formerly Allen Avery, abutting south *[was this a copyist's mistake for 'north'?]* on the Sutton footway and extending north and south to plough lands on the same shott . . . formerly occupied by Thomas Arden" *[who had owned The Old Farm and whose estate had largely passed to Edward Carleton]* In the marriage settlement made in 1763 by Samuel Swinfen's heir, Thomas Ball, the item "One piece of land called the Chalk Pit. 1 acre" appears to be relevant; especially as, when the Ball family in 1787, sold their Carshalton land to Samuel Long, the conveyance included: "A piece of land called the West Piece with a Chalk Pit, abutting east and west on lands of George Taylor, north on Lower Road and enclosed land of George Taylor, south on a certain footway from Carshalton to Sutton." Those 4 acres certainly correspond with the 'shott' of which, in 1716, the chalk pit formed part, but the 'certain footway' seems to have been very uncertainly located. As well as this 4 acre holding Samuel Long also acquired by the same conveyance, *inter alia*, "1 acre in Pear Tree Shott *[seemingly the 1839 "Inn Peartree"]*, abutting east on land of Theodore Henry Broadhead *[the current owner of Carshalton House]*; . . . and 1 acre, part of common lands lying in Chalk Pit Hill, abutting east and south on land of George Taylor . . . north on land of Theodore Henry Broadhead."

Apparently connected with the copyhold land included in Lots III, IV and V of the 1839 auction, are references Sister Pauline Stevens found in the present deeds of Carshalton House to "2 acres of customary *[i.e. copyhold]* land in the Common Fields of Carshalton: 1 acre called The Piece by the Old Chalk Pit, shooting East and West, lying between the Chalk Pit formerly of Thomas Balls *[sic]*, then Thomas Walpole *[owner of Carshalton House from 1767 to 1782]* . . . and the Carshalton to Sutton highway, and abutting on land formerly of Thomas Scawen *[whose lordship of the manor was later bought by George Taylor]* . . . On the north, and on land of Thomas Balls, then Thomas Walpole on the south. *[The other acre was on the south side of the "said highway" so was not connected with the Chalk Pit]* . . . which 2 acres were formerly in the tenure or occupation of Richard Garrard *[that must have been before Thomas Ball's time]*, then of

Clement Kynnersley decd. *[owner of Carshalton House from 1805 to 1816]* , then of William Foster Reynolds *[Kynnersley's successor]* ."

It is obvious that conveyancers often found it very difficult to keep track of all the owners of real estate in Carshalton — not surprisingly, since old-time gentlemen bought, sold and split up land holdings just as their modern counterparts do their investment portfolios of stocks and shares. But the Chalk Pit referred to in all these documents is clearly the one which now accommodates the houses in Rossdale. And the constantly mentioned footpath in its vicinity was still shown on the Tithe map of 1847, skirting the chalk pit at its northern end. But that ancient route to Sutton disappeared in 1853 when an Inclosure Award put Carshalton's remaining common fields into private ownership and stopped up all the old rights of way which had existed in them for access purposes. (This footpath to Sutton had probably run into Manor Lane which was originally a footpath from Sutton to Carshalton.)

It is not known when Carshalton House's Chalk Pit ceased to be worked. After local builders had stopped using chalk blocks in houses, the material was still quarried for burning to manufacture lime. Trade directories show that that industry was carried on in Carshalton until, at least, the middle of the 19th century; but the exact location of the lime kilns is not stated. It is significant, though, that the present Carshalton House deeds, which seem to date from 1839, refer to "The Piece by the Old Chalk Pit", suggesting that the latter was not then being worked.

THE BRICKFIELD

The present-day Brookfield Avenue was, until modern houses were built along it, called Brickfield Lane. Our ancestors had a preference for realistic rather than fanciful nomenclature. Brickfield Lane had been so named because of the brickfield on its west side, which once went with Carshalton House. Old maps show the original road to have been a cul-de-sac, and its sole purpose would seem to have been to enable the products of the brickfield to be removed on wheeled vehicles.

Among the Carleton properties conveyed to Sir John Fellowes in 1716 was a "Close of land called Spartmore, containing 8 acres, being the middle close of land formerly called or known by the name of Spartmore, being the furthest from the town of Carshalton of the said three closes formerly called Spartmore containing 7 acres. *[There seems to be a mistake in the wording of this.]* These last two closes are commonly now called Brickfield." In the 1732 conveyance of Sir John's estate by his nephew, Coulson Fellowes, to Samuel Swinfen, the description of this item of property is in similar terms, confused though they appear to be. But, in 1763, when Thomas Ball, Samuel Swinfen's heir, settled his Carshalton holdings on his future wife, there was included "One close of land called the Brickfield, containing 15 acres". It looks from this as though there was a copyist's error at one time and what Sir John Fellowes actually acquired was two closes containing respectively 8 acres and 7 acres which together were known as the Brickfield. The position was made even clearer when Samuel Long, in 1787, bought the Ball family's Carshalton land, including "2 pieces of ground in the meadow commonly called Spartmore's Brick Field, being near a lane or road called Spartmore's Lane, containing 14 acres, 1 rood, 3 poles, occupied by James King, undertenant to Samuel Wallace."

Spartmore Lane was an old name for the present Wrythe Lane. It is shown as Sparkmore Lane on the 'Arundel' map, but, while the 1787 conveyance was calling it roughly that, to Carshalton's Vestry it was Spartelmy Green Lane. In 1484, however, it had appeared in the Court Rolls as "Sparkinge Lane near le Rye"; and a little earlier they had mentioned 3 crofts called "Spectmore's", while, on one occasion the name "Sparkman's Green" was given to Wrythe Green, and, on another occasion, it was called "Spartling Green". It is easy enough to say that our ancestors didn't know how to spell; but the trouble probably was that they didn't pronounce their words clearly, so that conveyancers and other scribes had great difficulty in making out strange place names proferred in local dialects – not to mention the subsequent difficulty of reading correctly what had been made of the sounds by another practitioner of the art of writing.

As a business, the other Carshalton brickfield off Green Wrythe Lane was, judging by late 18th century rating valuations, similar in size to the one off Brick-field Lane; but the latter kept going for much longer, being still active in the early part of this century. However, after its sale in 1732, it never again became part of the Carshalton House estate; and how or when it originally came into the posses-sion of Edward Carleton does not appear from the available documents.

THE SWAN INN

This West Street building, at present empty after having been, for a large part of this century, the premises of a timber merchant, ceased to be a public house about 1909, but had been in the 'licensed trade' for centuries before that. Exactly how long, nobody knows. The inhabitants of West Street would, however, have needed from quite early times the social amenity of an alehouse much nearer to them than the High Street of Carshalton. And an alehouse more than an inn was what the 'Swan' originally was. (It took its name, presumably, from the wild life on the water which once, nearby, filled the mouth of West Street.)

From its situation, with the park of Carshalton House immediately to the south and west of it, one would have expected the 'Swan Inn' (as it was eventually called) to have belonged always to the owner of that mansion. But it does not figure in the 1716 conveyance of Edward Carleton's property to Sir John Fellowes. Nevertheless the latter had evidently acquired it by 1721, in which year the statement of assets he rendered to the Parliamentary Committee investigating the collapse of the South Sea Company included the item: "An inn or alehouse with some lands let to Richard Grandy". Somewhat surprisingly, these premises do not appear to have been purchased in the 1732 sale of Sir John's estate either by Sir Philip Yorke, who bought Carshalton House, or by Samuel Swinfen, who bought most of the remaining former Carleton properties. For the 'Swan Inn' next appears in the Court Rolls in the ownership of the Reverend William Hollier, Car-shalton's rector from 1703 to 1738, who, from his bedroom windows in the Old Rectory, would have been able to keep a supervisory eye on his acquisition.

After Hollier's death, what was described in the Court Rolls as "The Old Swan Alehouse" was sold by his nephew for £210 to Richard Garrard, father-in-law of the next rector, Edmund Lodge. Then, in 1771, the same record has an entry relating to its transfer to the Hon. Thomas Walpole, who, four years earlier, had bought Carshalton House. But the next owner of that property, Theodore Broadhead, took over from Walpole "the messuage heretofore called The Old Swan Alehouse, but which, together with the old buildings thereunto belonging, have been taken down and another Messuage and Buildings erected in their stead", to quote from a land deed in the Surrey Record Office. How long the resuscitated 'Swan' remained with Carshalton House I have been unable to discover. But it was not mentioned in the sale catalogue of 1839 when the mansion and its lands were auctioned by the executors of William Foster Reynolds.

This humble alehouse seems, in the 18th century, to have provided an apprenticeship for aspiring innkeepers. In the late 1700s John Drayton was its rated occupier, and he went on to the 'Greyhound' in 1801. William Mansell had been running it when the Hon. Thomas Walpole acquired it, and he later turns up as 'mine host' of the 'King's Arms'. And Richard Grandy, who was its tenant in Sir John Fellowes's time, is next recorded (under the name Richard Grande) as the landlord of the 'Greyhound'. That early 18th century innkeeper was remarkably long-lived for his time, being 92 years of age when he died in 1736. His tombstone shows, in addition, that his wife had died in 1725 at the age of 63, having borne him five sons and nine daughters. He had been well on in years when he left the 'Old Swan', but evidently it had been an irresistible temptation to move from a humble alehouse to what James Edwards in *A Companion from London to Brightelmston'* was later to call "a large and good accustomed inn".

LOWER MILL

As its name indicates, this was once Carshalton's only other mill besides Upper Mill, the first to be established. When Domesday Book was compiled there was one solitary mill in the manor — almost certainly built near the site of the last-known Upper Mill, which was in the grounds of the present-day 'Stone Court'. Lower Mill itself undoubtedly dates back to the later Middle Ages when it seems to have been called 'Chamberlayne's Mill'. But the first particularised description we have of it comes from the 1716 conveyance to Sir John Fellowes of Edward Carleton's estate. Lower Mill appears in that as "a mill, formerly a Water Griest Mill, called Burton Mill, now used for and as a Copper Mill". With it there went "10 acres of meadow ground abutting on the river" and also "free liberty of fishing in the Common Stream there." The description concludes: "This mill and ground were formerly occupied by Walter Stiles, late occupied by John Morris." (The last mill on the site still stands, much altered, in the premises of Vinyl Products.)

The name "Burton Mill" suggests how Edward Carleton might have come into possession of it. Dixey Longe had bought the half of the Carshalton manor which had belonged to the Burtons, and his widow married Thomas Arden, whose estate, by some undiscovered transaction, passed largely into Carleton's ownership. The mill changed from grinding corn to beating copper into sheets probably as a result of the late 17th century introduction into England of a Dutch method of producing a material much used at the time for manufacturing domestic utensils. 'The Copper Mill' was still engaged in this industry when, in 1726, to get the Vestry's permission for the erection in the Church of a memorial to Sir John

124

Fellowes, his brother and heir, Edward, placed on the premises a charge of £20 a year for the benefit of the poor of the parish. The indenture (a copy of which is in the Surrey Record Office) specifies the land going with the "Water Copper Mill" as 3 acres of orchard on the east and west of it and a 6 acre meadow which seems identifiable with the land on the east bank of the river below Butter Hill bridge, later to be made into a bleaching ground for the calico printing works established in Lower Mill after it had ceased to pound copper into shape. But, long before that happened, the owners of Carshalton House had ceased to have any interest in the property. Presumably, Coulson Fellowes sold it in 1732 with the rest of his uncle's estate, but it does not appear in his conveyance to Samuel Swinfen. Whether or not it was bought by Sir Philip Yorke (later Lord Hardwicke), the purchaser of Carshalton House itself, is impossible to say, because the conveyance to him has not come to light. All one can say for certain is that Lower Mill next appears, in the middle of the 18th century, in the ownership of Thomas Scawen, the current lord of the manor.

The subsequent history of the premises is well documented, but not relevant to the story of Carshalton House. However, without the charge made on them for the benefit of the Fellowes Charity — still being paid by the current owners in the early part of this century — it would have been much more difficult to establish such a certain identification of Lower Mill as is now possible.

THE MALTINGS

Amongst the freehold Carleton properties conveyed to Sir John Fellowes in 1716 were: "a Messuage or tenement with appurtenances, part of which is used for and as a Malthouse"; "30 acres of freehold lands with walnut trees, formerly of Thomas Hawkins, late of Robert Hawkins"; and "a Little cottage and backside occupied by Nicholas Gawen". In the statement of assets which Sir John submitted to Parliament in 1721, he referred to these items as "A house, malthouse, outhouses and lands in the common field let to Robert Hawkins" and "a Thacht House and Orchard let to Nicholas Going." Under the heading: "Messuage and 30 acres with walnut trees and a cottage and backside in the tenure of Nicholas Gawen in Carshalton, Wallington and Beddington", the deeds of Samuel Long's estate (in the Surrey Record Office) mention a mortgage with endorsements which show that Edward Carleton, in 1709, had bought from Thomas Best, in all, "a cottage, 40 acres of land, 5 acres of meadow and 10 acres of pasture, with appurtenances, in Wallington, Carshalton and Beddington." These particulars were given in support of the title acquired by Samuel Swinfen from Coulson Fellowes to the following properties which had formerly belonged to Sir John Fellowes: "A messuage or tenement with appurtenances (part used as a malthouse). Freehold lands containing 30 acres with walnut trees, formerly possessed by Thomas Hawkins. A cottage and backside of Nicholas Gawen. All, except the cottage and backside, occupied by Robert Hawkins." (It appears from this that the malthouse and the house which went with it came into existence after Edward Carleton's purchase in 1709).

Samuel Swinfen's heir, Thomas Ball, included in the Carshalton real estate he settled, in 1763, on his intended wife: "All that messuage or tenement and the Maltings and Malthouse being in Carshalton, and all those lands containing 30 acres in the parish and fields of Carshalton and the hamlet of Wallington, the premises then tenanted or occupied by William Heath." But neither this property nor the cottage and backside passed to Samuel Long when he bought the Ball family's Carshalton holdings in 1787. Those two items are not, in fact, traceable in any other conveyance which is available for public inspection. However, from the details given in the legal documents already cited, it is possible to make an almost certain identification of both the premises in question. The 30 acres of land attached to them evidently extended into Wallington, and the only place fronting on a road where there could have been any such holding in the 18th century was the north side of Westcroft Road, towards its eastern end. The Westcroft field at the west end of the road is stated, in other conveyances, to have contained 8 acres, but, east of that, the land is unaccounted for in available deeds if it is not the 30 acres which went with the maltings, the maltster's house and the cottage.

There are further circumstances which support this identification. A Carshalton rate book which ends in 1767 shows an assessment that year on "William Heath, Moltster". The next rate book which has been preserved begins in 1782 and by then the malting business appears to have been given up; but there is an assessment on "Mr. Beynon, late Heath". Edward Beynon had married the sister and heiress of Stephen Heath, and in 1785 he built a mansion called 'Parkfields' on the north side of Westcroft Road near the Wallington boundary. (It was there until shortly before the First World War, but was then pulled down.) Edward Beynon died in 1801, leaving to his wife, not only 'Parkfields', but also "the messuage, tenement or [? should be "and"] cottage adjoining thereunto, with the appurtenances, now in the occupation of the Rev. Mr. Walker". The rate books show that the house in which this clergyman lived was the one on which, in 1782, "Mr. Beynon, late Heath" had been assessed.

All the evidence, then, points to this having been the residence of William Heath the 'Moltster'. A substantially built old house, which has been given the name of 'Parkfields', still stands near the site of the former mansion of that name. And it surely cannot be just a chance coincidence that, adjoining it, there is an old cottage (now called 'Parkfields Lodge'). It is not thatched, but otherwise it corresponds with the one occupied in the early 18th century by Nicholas Gowan (alias Going). How much of the original fabric remains in the present-day 'Parkfields' and 'Parkfields Lodge' is a question for experts to speculate on. It is pretty clear, though, that the 30 acre walnut plantation which once went with them and stretched into Wallington, now carries, not trees, but the numerous small houses built in this century along the north side of Westcroft Road and on both sides of the comparatively modern Caledon Road.

OTHER PROPERTIES

In addition to the 'messuages' already mentioned, there were also listed, in the statement of assets delivered by Sir John Fellowes to Parliament in 1721, the following dwelling houses situated in Carshalton:
(1)   "An old House and Outhouses, much out of repair and uninhabited, and 17 or 18 acres of land in my possession being part of what was formerly let with the last mentioned House". This property is not identifiable in any subsequent conveyance, and no indication of its whereabouts is obtainable.

(2)   Five small tenements which seem to constitute the following item in the 1716 conveyance of former Carleton property: "Messuage, Barns, Stables, Outhouses etc. in Carshalton, formerly occupied by Walter Stiles, reconverted to five tenements . . . formerly the estate of David Otgher and Martha, his wife, or one of them . . . ." Martha Otgher was Edward Carleton's cousin and he was the executor of her will made in 1706. In the *Peatling Papers* there is a note that the Otghers lived in the Old Rectory, but no authority for this statement is given. From very slender indications, I think it more likely that their house was near the site of The Lodge, but no positive identification of the premises described in the conveyance of 1716 is possible. They seem to have been on their last legs at that time, having been subjected to the indignity of being subdivided into five tenements. At any rate, I have found no further mention of them in any available document.

(3)   "A very old house and some lands in the common field let to Robert Bruce and William Buckstone". This also has disappeared without trace, and no clue to its address has survived.

(4)   "A Farm let to Thomas Hickson". This figured in the 1716 conveyance as a messuage with 19½ acres called Stiles Meadows; it was still in the occupation of Thomas Hickson in 1732 when sold by Coulson Fellowes to Samuel Swinfen. The property does not seem to have passed to Thomas Ball, Swinfen's heir, and I have not discovered what happened to it or where it was.

As well as his 'messuages', Sir John Fellowes, by 1721, also owned in Carshalton "39 acres of meadow or pasture ground" together with a number of arable holdings in the common fields. These latter have picturesque names and some can be identified as having been acquired by Samuel Long in 1787. It might be possible, too, from the Inclosure Award of 1853, to get some idea of their respective locations. But what would be the point of going to such trouble? They all now lie incognito under the houses and shops and roads in that part of the old manor on which, in this century, the name 'Carshalton Beeches' has mistakenly been conferred.

Edward Carleton had acquired a very considerable area of Carshalton, partly out of the 'Manor of Kinnersley' and partly out of the half of the manor of Carshalton, bought by Dixey Longe, bequeathed to his widow and passed to Thomas Arden, her second husband. Sir John Fellowes increased the Carleton holdings slightly. But, after his ultimate heir, Coulson Fellowes, had sold the Carshalton property in two parts, the real estate owned by subsequent possessors of the mansion was mainly confined to its immediate vicinity. Before the South Sea Bubble burst, Sir John had seemed likely to rival the lord of the manor, Sir William Scawen, as a local property tycoon. The 18th century successors to the Fellowes brothers in Carshalton House were satisfied to draw their wealth from the City of London and did not challenge the Scawens, the Bynes and the Longs as Carshalton landowners. (William Foster Reynolds, in the early part of the 19th century, added a large part of the 'Long' estate to his Carshalton House holdings, but it was separately disposed of after his death.)

BOOKS MENTIONED IN THE TEXT

AUBREY, John. The natural history and antiquities of the County of Surrey. Begun in the year 1673 . . . 5 volumes, 1718-1719. Facsimile reprint, Dorking, Kohler & Coombes, 1975.

BARRETT, Charles R. B. Surrey: highways, byways and waterways. Bliss, Sands & Foster, 1895.

BRAYLEY, Edward W. A topographical history of Surrey. 5 vols. Robert Best Ede, 1841. Revised edition by Edward Walford, 4 vols, Virtue [1878].

BRIGHTLING, George B. Some particulars relating to the history and antiquities of Carshalton . . . 1st edition 1872. 2nd edition 1882. Facsimile reprint with added index of the 2nd edition published by Sutton Libraries & Arts Services, 1978.

DICTIONARY OF NATIONAL BIOGRAPHY. Founded in 1882 by George Smith. Published in 22 volumes 1908-9 with supplements to 1960.

EDWARDS, James. Companion from London to Brightelmston, 2nd ed. [1801].

FIELD, H. *and* BUNNEY, M. English domestic architecture of the XVIIth and XVIIIth centuries. Bell, 1905.

JONES, A. E. From medieval manor to London suburb: an obituary of Carshalton. Carshalton, published by the author, 1970.

JONES, A. E. An illustrated directory of old Carshalton. Carshalton, published by the author, 1973.

LYSONS, Daniel. The environs of London: being an historical account of the towns, villages, and hamlets within twelve miles of the Capital. 1st ed. 5 vols., 1792-80 supplement 1811.

MANNING, *Rev.* Owen *and* BRAY, William. The history and antiquities of the County of Surrey. 3 vols, 1804-14; facsimile edition EP Publishing and Surrey County Library, 1974.

NAMIER, *Sir* Lewis *and* BROOKE, John. The history of Parliament: The House of Commons 1754-1790. 3 vols. HMSO, 1964.

O'CALLAGHAN, *Sir* Desmond D. T. Guns, gunners and others, Chapman and Hall, 1925.

SEDGWICK, Romney. The history of Parliament: The House of Commons 1715-1745. 2 vols. HMSO, 1970.

VICTORIA history of the County of Surrey; edited by H. E. Malden. 4 vols. First published 1902; re-issued Dawsons, for the University of London Institute of Historical Research, 1967.

VICTORIA history of the County of Huntingdonshire; edited by William Page. First published 1926. Dawsons, for the University of London Institute of Historical Research, 1974.

'The Peatling Papers' is an unpublished work relating to Carshalton local history, compiled by Dr. A. V. Peatling [c. 1902-1922]. Original in Sutton Central Library Archives; photocopies available for use in Sutton, Carshalton and Wallington Libraries. 14 volumes with index.

INDEX

(Note: illustrations are indicated by page numbers in **bold** type)

CHRONOLOGICAL LIST OF THE KNOWN OWNERS AND OCCUPIERS OF CARSHALTON HOUSE

The Old Farm
Bartholomew Kynardsley
Edward Burton
John Scott
John Scott (younger)
Scott brothers
Sir Edward Herbert
Dixey Longe
Thomas Arden
Edward Carleton

Carshalton House: early 18th century
Edward Carleton
Dr Radcliffe
Sir John Fellowes

Carshalton House: later 18th century
Edward Fellowes
Coulson Fellowes
Hardwicke, *1st Earl of*
William Mitchell (the elder)
Elizabeth Mitchell
William Mitchell (the younger)

Lord Anson
Sir George Amyand
Dame Anna Maria Amyand
Hon. Thomas Walpole
Theodore Henry Broadhead
John Hodson Durand

Carshalton House: 19th century owners/occupiers
David Mitchell
Clement Kynnersley
William Foster Reynolds
Edward Simeon
Ordnance School
Edmund Batt
Albert Pelly
Dr Alfred Barrett
Charles Barrett
The Daughters of the Cross

Carshalton House: 20th century
The Daughters of the Cross (St Philomena's)